To Touch The World
The Peace Corps Experience

The Peace Corps wishes to express its appreciation to the authors and publishers for their permission to reprint the following pieces: "Everyone Everywhere Has Tales to Tell" by Carol Severance, © 1994; "George Brett's Batting Average?" by Dwight Wilson, © 1994, reprinted from *RPCV Writers & Readers*; "Development Is Down This Road" by Abigail Calkins, © 1992, reprinted from *RPCV Writers & Readers*; "Kalahari Desert: Sunset" by Christopher Conlon, © 1994; "Letter From Poland" by Mary Melinda Ziemer, © 1992, reprinted from *RPCV Writers & Readers*; "Shakespeare in Calabar" by Tom Hebert, © 1992, reprinted from *RPCV Writers & Readers*; "The Song of Our People" by David Arnold, © 1993, reprinted from *RPCV Writers & Readers*; "Raid on Entebbe, or My Three Days as a Mercenary" by Tina Thuermer, © 1994, reprinted from *RPCV Writers & Readers*; "I Had A Hero" by Mike Tidwell, © 1990, reprinted from *The Ponds of Kalambayi: An African Sojourn*, Lyons and Burford Publishers; "From Leningrad to Budapest" by Jeffrey Taylor, © 1994, reprinted from *RPCV Writers & Readers*; "Learning the African Protocols" by Denise Voelker, © 1993, reprinted from *Emergency*

Magazine; "So This Is Paris" by Kathleen Coskran, © 1994, reprinted from *RPCV Writers & Readers*; "Hearts and Minds" by P.F. Kluge, © 1991, reprinted from *The Edge of Paradise,* Random House; "The Mending Fields" by Bob Shacochis, © 1994; "Mariama" by Susan Rich, © 1994; "At Home In The World" by Bill Moyers, © 1994; "But No Postcards" by John Coyne, © 1993, reprinted from *RPCV Writers and Readers.*

For more information about the Peace Corps please call
800-424-8580.

January 1995

Library of Congress Catalog No. 94-74153
ISBN 0-9644472-0-7

To Touch The World
The Peace Corps Experience

Peace Corps acknowledges the efforts of John Coyne, Suzy Becker, Elizabeth McAlee, Louis Welton, and Rose Green in the selection, editing, design and production of this book.

CONTENTS

INTRODUCTION

A Call To Serve

by Carol Bellamy

Throughout time, there have been many eloquent calls to service. In his inaugural address, John F. Kennedy, who founded the Peace Corps, spoke words that many in my generation have taken to heart: "... ask not what your country can do for you—ask what you can do for your country ... ask not what America can do for you, but together what we can do for the freedom of man."

A call to serve can take many forms—something you hear or read or see. You can't respond to every call, but in your lifetime there will be at least one that really pricks your conscience, that moves you to action. For over 140,000 Americans—including me—that call came from the Peace Corps.

Bill Moyers, once deputy director of the Peace Corps and now a contributor to this collection, sums up why people join. "It was said that the urge to join the Peace Corps was passion alone. Not so. Men and women, whatever their age, looked their lives over and chose to affirm. To affirm is the thing. And so they have—in quiet, self-effacing perseverance."

In the three decades it has spanned, Peace Corps has held a special attraction for Americans—a way of serving their country, and a way of helping others. Peace Corps Volunteers are different from other Americans who go overseas. They are not missionaries. Or tourists. They are not intelligence agents, or academics. They are not there on business trips or to advise foreign governments.

Peace Corps Volunteers are invited by developing countries to come and share their skills. They live the way the people in that country live—not in big houses, or behind high walls. They don't have servants or fancy cars. In fact, they don't have their own car at all.

Most visitors to developing countries will never venture outside of the capital city or an isolated vacation spot. Peace Corps Volunteers live and work in villages and cities that may never be tourist sites, and towns at the ends of the earth. They unpack their belongings. They settle down. They set about to do a job. And they make some lifelong friends along the way.

In many of the essays you're about to read, you will see how Peace Corps changed the lives of these Volunteers. Tom Peirce, for example, writing about being a Togo Volunteer a few years ago, said, "It is no longer possible for me to think of the world in the abstract geopolitical terms my academic career had taught. Rather, I am aware of the complex maze of cultures and the challenge of bridging them together."

The same was true for me. My Peace Corps experience in Guatemala thirty years ago was the most profound and eye-opening education I have ever had. I will forever be aware of the problems and possibilities of other nations, of other peoples in those nations. Two years in the Peace Corps also taught me a lot about myself. As a Peace Corps Volunteer, you find out you're more adaptable, a little tougher and more resilient than you thought.

The Peace Corps prepares new Volunteers for their work abroad. You learn a language, and are given training that helps you learn what to expect and what to do when the unexpected happens. Also, Volunteers have the support of an American staff overseas, wherever they are in the world.

Peace Corps Volunteers serve in over ninety countries around the world—in Asia, Latin America, the Pacific, Africa, the Middle East, Eastern and Central Europe, and the former Soviet Union. There are Peace Corps projects in Benin and Yemen, Madagascar and Micronesia, Czech Republic and Chile. Volunteers are working in nations that are just making it onto the map: Kazakhastan and Kyrghyzstan. They're also in Uzbekistan and Moldova and Turkmenistan.

They're working on education, business development, and the environment. They are working in health and agriculture. But, as many schools and roads and wells as Volunteers have built, perhaps the most important thing that they have built is hope. It's a very American sensibility—to think that with hard work you can improve your life. And, it's a very Peace Corps sensibility to go out and actually help people do it.

With all the problems and challenges facing us today, one person's work may seem like a drop in the bucket, but I think Robert Kennedy said it best: "Few will have the greatness to bend history itself, but each of us can work to change a small portion of events, and in the total of all those acts will be written the history of this generation."

What you have here, then, is history—with many more generations still to be written.

Carol Bellamy (Guatemala 1963-65) is the first returned Peace Corps Volunteer to be named director of the agency. Prior to being appointed Peace Corps Director, she was an investment banker, as well as a New York State Senator and the first woman President of the New York City Council. She graduated from Gettysburg College and has a law degree from New York University. She is also a former Fellow at the Institute of Politics of the Kennedy School of Government at Harvard University.

Washington, D.C.

The Cure Is Care

by R. Sargent Shriver

The Peace Corps gave me the most memorable, continuing, morally unblemished, and uncompromised chance ever given any American to serve his country, his countrymen, and his fellow human beings worldwide, simultaneously, and at the grassroots level with the poor everywhere.

Never in war, and I have served in war; never in peace, and I have served in many places in peace, has anyone ever received, from a secular state, a greater opportunity for pure service.

I was privileged to be part of a great band of people. From among the Volunteers who served overseas when I was director have come senators, congressmen, directors of overseas programs both public and private, foreign service officers, bankers, congressional staff members, state government officials, city mayors, and on and on. The Peace Corps proved to be the best talent agency for public servants in this century of American history.

Despite this, can there be optimism now for the future of the Peace Corps?

The Peace Corps budget is only 3/100,000 of the Defense Department's. Its numbers are only 3/1,000 of the Armed Forces. One thousand men and women are enrolled to serve our needs in war for every three—repeat three—in the Peace Corps. Talk about David and Goliath! By any quantitative measure known to the Rand Corporation, the American Enterprise Institute, or Office of Management and Budget, the Peace Corps is almost inconsequential, irrelevant perhaps, a cipher in the great game of world politics and power.

Then why are we here—two thousand of us attending this anniversary celebration[The Twentieth Anniversary of the Peace Corps, in 1981]?

Are we grown men and women but still talking about juvenile things? Are we just on a nostalgia kick? Are we puerile romantics, idealists, flower children, merely tolerated by mature, realistic, worldly wise leaders? Are we just accepted because all human societies have their soft-headed dreamers, their physically crippled and mentally retarded, their psychologically immature? Aren't the draft and military service the best way to deal with Peace Corps Volunteer types, past, present, and future? Wouldn't the draft teach Peace Corps people to shape up, learn about the real world, guarantee their passage from illusion to realism? Can we as a nation, in difficult economic times, spend taxpayers' dollars on such a whimsical, peripheral activity as a corps dedicated to peace?

Many experts today say no. They say we should not dissipate our national resources and strength. Government was not established, they say, to create, finance, or direct such activities. The "private sector" is the proper place for idealistic experiments. The Peace Corps has little or nothing to do, they say, with our Constitutional purposes to create a more perfect union, establish justice, provide for the common defense, promote the general welfare, and secure the blessings of liberty for ourselves and our posterity. The Peace Corps, it is alleged, does not contribute to the defense of the United States. It does not protect the people from dangers abroad or at home. It's a misplaced, vestigial remainder of a messianic culture of the past. Good, perhaps, for Mormons, Mennonites, Quakers, left-wing Catholics, Pacifists, Evangelicals —but only a sideshow in an era controlled by the hard sciences, technology, finance, economics, and military matters. The threat is from without, not from within; from the U.S.S.R., not from ourselves. We're all right; they're all wrong; and we will prove it by our strength. The Peace Corps has little or no role in dealing with the real threat to America.

Thoughts like these may predominate in many places today, but the Peace Corps is always full of surprises, and happiness, and *truth*.

I experienced that joy and that truth all over again when I met again Beulah Bartlett and Blythe Monroe, two of our first PCVs to Ethiopia. Those two women were 68 and 66 when they volunteered for the Peace Corps, and yesterday they both received tumultuous applause for their work and their spirit. They inspired us all—just by their presence on the platform.

After they left the stage, Beulah looked up at me and said, "You saved my life."

What a lovely thing for her to say, I thought. It was beautiful...but, of course, it wasn't true!

I never saved Beulah's life. Beulah saved her own life by giving it away. She offered it to service. Her gift of herself to the poor and uneducated in Ethiopia gave her a new lease on a new life...a life of service and peace.

The Peace Corps is thousands of human beings at peace—with themselves, with their fellow man, with the world. Why? Because they have saved their own lives. How? By giving themselves away!!

We never own anything till we give it away. That's the heart of peace; that's the heart of the Peace Corps.

When will we learn that truth, here in our beloved U.S.A., the land of conspicuous consumption and wealth?

We must learn it...without tragedy or suffering to teach it to us, if possible, because it has the power to save our lives—just as it saved Beulah's.

I used the word power just then. I used it on purpose—I used it to emphasize the power of peace. It is peace that gives strength. It is peace that provides "the force"—an unconquerable, unsurpassable force...not arms, not bombs, not fear or threat of destruction. Those things just arouse resistance and resentment. They produce the opposite of what they intend. The alleged "power of arms" is a sham. The man with the pistol in his hand blazing away is the pitiful, fearful weakling afraid of another person, killing and marauding like a frustrated child because he's angry and hurt and alone and desperate, looking for love and finding only hatred and opposition. No, I never saved Beulah's life or Blythe's life. They saved themselves...because they learned to give themselves away...as the Declaration of Independence says in its last and most important words: "We pledge our lives, our fortunes, and our sacred honor." Risking their lives, giving their fortunes, and themselves, the original American Revolutionaries found peace.

That's why I am less confused and more knowledgeable and realistic about peace than in 1960 when we began the Peace Corps. In the 1960s we thought it would be easy. We thought Congress would always increase our size and our budget, if we produced results.

We thought we could defeat poverty, enlighten the ignorant, eradicate disease, win over our enemies, given enough time, given enough Volunteers. Now I know different, not better, but deeper. I know we still need money and Volunteers. I know the U.S.A. and the world needs the Peace Corps. But now I think we can achieve peace without eradicating poverty or ignorance or disease. The "power of peace" does not lie in the vain hope that we can change the human condition everywhere and for everyone. Our

American faith in a technological fix for every problem is naive and irrelevant. Millions of people don't want our technology, our culture, our values. They've heard promises about a materialistic heaven on earth from communists and capitalists. Great improvements in the materialistic conditions of life are promised by both. But neither system has ever produced anything but an imposed peace—which is peace only for the mighty, and not even pure peace for them. Look how rich men and Politburo members employ guards and guard dogs, TV monitors, and elaborate alarm systems to protect themselves and their possessions and positions. The leader of the free world, ironically, needs more protection than anyone, except the leader of the communist world.

Those men are not creating or enjoying peace; they are creating and enjoying power. Augustus Caesar, the greatest of Roman Emperors, built a Temple of Peace—but only after he had gained absolute power. He encouraged people to worship him, the state he had created, the armies that sustained them. Deus, Imperator, Rex—God, Emperor, Leader. Augustus had it all! But was it peace?

Jesus Christ said no. And the Christians had to go underground—because they worshiped a different God. They threatened the stability of the kingdom of Augustus by declaring that another kingdom exists...a kingdom where peace comes from below, from the ground up, not from the top down, from inside the hearts of human beings, not from the barrel of a gun no matter who's holding it.

Many Peace Corps Volunteers have possessed this kind of power. They were at peace with themselves and with their work. That's why the Peace Corps nurses in the Dominican Republic were asked to stay when the revolutionary slogans all said "Yankees Go Home." That's why no Peace Corps Volunteers were attacked or injured in the Panamanian uprisings against the U.S.A. in 1964 or during the 1981 violence in El Salvador. That's why "terrorists" have not assaulted Peace Corps Volunteers even in remote locations in the underdeveloped world.

Certainly there have been accidents. Surely there will be deaths. PCVs could get killed just as the nuns were killed in El Salvador, just as priests, missionaries and others sometimes get killed—overseas or here at home.

But the peace of the Peace Corps Volunteers is not something that can be taken from them, even by death. It's a peace they can give endlessly because giving it away does not diminish the supply.

Expressed differently, it's the quality of caring—caring for others, willingness, even eagerness, to teach the ignorant or bathe the dirty, nurse the leper, or serve as a farmer, lawyer, doctor, technician, nurses' aide in places where thousands, even millions, need what you have, in skills, yes, but most of all in human warmth.

No free market can ever replace free human services rendered by one free human being to another human being. A "good society" is the result of billions of such good acts. Government is good, not overreaching or intrusive, when government encourages, supports, and facilitates good, moral activity by the citizens. We are being swamped, night and day, with propaganda for selfishness, for excessive consumption, for killing, for domination of peoples, of nature, of history.

Is it too much to ask ourselves, we who believe in the Peace Corps, is it too much to ask ourselves?

Shouldn't we swing back into action? Shouldn't we volunteer again?

How should we begin? Exactly the way human beings always begin—by organizing ourselves. Into what? Into "communities of caring."

In Latin America, basic caring communities have been started right in the villages. Those are caring communities—people caring for one another. That's what Peace Corps administrators meant in 1960 when we talked about community development—developing a sense of community spirit, community action at the grassroots or the rice roots. That's why Americans with only a bachelor's degree were sought after and sent abroad. We were looking for caring people, not just curing people, those able to cure a disease or a problem. Sure we wanted curing people, but only if they were caring people, too.

In a phrase, the cure is care. Caring for others is the practice of peace! Caring becomes as important as curing. Caring produces the cure, not the reverse. Caring about nuclear war and its victims is the beginning of a cure for our obsession with war. Peace does not come through strength. Quite the opposite: Strength comes through peace. The practices of peace strengthen us for every vicissitude.

The task is immense!

Twenty years ago we called it "the towering task." Well, my friends, in 1981, "the towering task" still towers before us; but, thank God, we still have the Corps of Peace—that body of human beings who know, and have known, that America's destiny is not to be policeman of the world, monarch of the world, Caesar, Imperator, Rex, or Deus. But servant—servant of people, servant of peace, saviors of humanity.

It's a big task. But it's fun; it's joy; it's the true pursuit of happiness! May you all grow young in the achievement of it.

Volunteer!!

R. Sargent Shriver (Director 1961-66) founded the Peace Corps under President Kennedy. Following his five years with the agency, he was the first Director of the Office of Economic Opportunity, which created VISTA, Head Start, and Job Corps among other anti-poverty programs. Later he served as U.S. Ambassador to France in the Johnson Administration. A graduate of Yale University and Yale Law School, Shriver served in the U.S. Navy for five years. He is now the Chairman of the Board of Special Olympics International. In 1994 he was presented with the Medal of Freedom by President Clinton. In 1981 at Howard University he delivered *The Cure Is Care* to the Second National Conference of Former Peace Corps Volunteers and Staff.

Guatemala, Central America

Thirteen-Week Wonders

by Chris Davis

The plane is full of Peace Corps trainees. Sixty of us altogether, on our way to Guatemala, and I am sure that I am the only one on board who is completely panicked. The last lines from the letter I had received the previous week from the training director plays over and over in my head: "Training is a demanding and stressful period as you learn a lot about yourself and how to function in a new language and a new culture. It is our goal to help as many trainees as possible reach the greatest state of preparedness in order to best serve the development needs of Guatemala." How will I be prepared to be a Peace Corps Volunteer with only thirteen weeks of training? I wonder: Who will prepare me? And for what, exactly? I am not sure I am ready to be prepared.

The training center is located in the city of Antigua, which sits in a valley between two volcanoes, Agua and Fuego (Water and Fire). Eucalyptus trees and flowers line the cobbled streets of Antigua and friendly people leisurely make their way through the town, which has been destroyed three times by earthquakes. The training center is a large, walled, self-contained compound on the outskirts of the city. Picture small classroom huts in the center of a soccer arena with roaming animals and terraced gardens—wooden beehives are stacked against the far wall and half-finished clay stoves and compost piles seem to be growing in the field. Trainees from the group before us still have four days left here, and as they hustle about, it occurs to me that they know what they are doing. They ignore us, the new kids on the block.

I am assigned to a family and am sent to find their house armed with my bags, vague directions, and a piece of paper bearing their name. I find the house easily and am greeted by a man and woman who are about my age. They each hold a baby. My room is half the house, which has been divided by a sheet. They stand and watch me unpack. They also sit and watch me eat. I am trying to force down what they give me, none of it recognizable to me. Some kind of fried vegetable and small pieces of meat. The mother smiles broadly at me, turns to slap one of her older kids, then smiles at me again. Since I am unaware that I have to be the one to stand first, we sit at the table for over three hours.

At the training center we are divided into groups of two and three to practice Spanish. We are told not to speak English while at the training center. Thirteen weeks without English? The teachers are from Antigua and show great patience with us. They know little English and we know less Spanish so we draw pictures and communicate with our hands. We are sent out individually into the city with a list of questions in Spanish to ask in the market, bus station, and to random people on the street. We are told not to come back until we have the answers. Eventually a rescue party of trainees finds me in the market trying to pantomime my way out of a confrontation. Apparently, I had asked a clerk to fight me when all I really wanted was to pay for toilet paper.

The staff at the training center is terrific. They encourage us to discuss our feelings and frustrations with them and each other. This is not a problem. The staff is made up of Americans, mostly former Peace Corps Volunteers, and Guatemalans. There are technical program trainers for each of the five programs we represent. My program is Agriculture and my technical trainer is Andy. Technical trainers also seem to be personal counselors for the trainees in their program. We are told that we trainees are responsible for one another. Between other trainees, especially those in my program, and the staff, I feel a strong network of support building around me.

What strikes me most in those first couple of weeks is the diversity of my classmates in training. Not racial diversity, though there is that, but the differences in personalities. I had assumed that Peace Corps Volunteers would be a certain type. Long hair, beads, etc. I imagined that I would be the conservative one. Not so. There are Volunteers of all ages and all with a different point of view. There's the cynic, the class clown, the know-it-all, the shy one, and on and on. There really is no defining a Peace Corps Volunteer. What is truly amazing is that we all work together and utilize our differences. I tell this to Andy, the trainer, and he gives me a knowing smile as if he has heard this a thousand times before.

I am doing things I never dreamed of. I wake at 6 a.m. for a full day of technical and language training. I cut the heads off chickens and skin rabbits. I learn how to evenly terrace mountainsides using an A-frame leveler I make out of two corn stalks, string, and a rock. I am shown how to build a fuel-efficient stove that burns cow chips. I spend half my time in Spanish class trying to roll my r's. The day ends at 6 p.m. and I may go out with other trainees for a beer or, more likely, go home and to bed. I am told to throw everything I think I know about other people out the window—that yes could mean no and no could mean yes. I learn that there is no polite way to refuse food or drink and that the thumbs up signal means something vulgar in Guatemala.

After several weeks, we trainees are in high gear. Our initial shock at this new world is settling and we start to focus on learning, and learning as a team. We build compost piles from animal manure, garbage, and ash. We learn to grow broccoli. Not just how to plant it but when to plant it, how to make the tools to plant it, when to cut it, how to cut it so it will grow back again, how to seed it, how to cook and eat it. Everything is a process and no steps are skipped in anything we do. We are told that the villagers we will be working with cannot go to the store and buy seed or fertilizer and that we must work only with the resources available to them. Does broccoli grow wild in the mountains, I wonder?

I am suddenly used to cold showers, not shaving on a daily basis, using few words to express myself, and walking. Lots of walking. We see the film *El Norte* that depicts, somewhat accurately, the abuse of Guatemalan Indians by the government. We visit Peace Corps Volunteers in the field to see their projects. The Volunteers are so confident and accepted by their communities. I wonder if it will ever be this way for me. We hear lectures by Guatemalans about the culture of their country. We are instructed about how to take care of ourselves physically and emotionally. For the first time in my life, I think about my health a lot. We get rabies shots and a plethora of others; some make me slightly ill. We are all on an emotional high. I am a child again, and everything is new and exciting as I am rediscovering all my senses, which have become dull with routine in the States.

One particular moment of discovery comes at around 2 a.m. one rainy night. I am sitting in the latrine with my first bout of dysentery, water bottle at my feet to avoid dehydration. The latrine is only partially covered so rain is coming down on me. A giant pig is rooting around somewhere in the dark behind me and I hold onto a piece of bamboo to scare it off if it gets too close. My head is down and one hand is clutched to the side of the latrine as I throw up between my legs. Suddenly, I hear a low rumble and the ground is shaking. I initially believe I am experiencing some symptom, but the ground is really moving as I see the small silhouetted house in front of me roll up and down. After the earthquake ends, the rain begins to subside somewhat and I am feeling slightly better. I smile to myself. I feel invincible.

The days run together as we trainees become empowered and in control of our lives in Guatemala. We are more confident and have learned an incredible amount in a short period of time. We have taken Spanish tests and have been quizzed about our technical knowledge. We are told that much learning will occur at our sites and that we will be called back to the training center for additional training, from time to time. Finally, we are given our location assignments. I am scared and excited but, unlike on the flight on the way to Guatemala, this time I feel remarkably less nauseated and prepared for just about anything.

Chris Davis (Guatemala 1987-89) was a youth development Volunteer and worked in five rural Guatemalan villages. Davis was editor of *The ID*, a Peace Corps Guatemala publication and currently works in the Peace Corps Press Office in Washington, D.C. He earned a BS in Journalism and Public Relations from Northern Arizona University in Flagstaff, Arizona.

Guinea-Bissau, West Africa

Cross Cultural Dialogue

by Roz Wollmering

I entered the school doors brimming with ideas, innovative teaching methods, and the desire to have an effect. Today was the first day of school in Guinea-Bissau, the tiny West African country where I had been assigned as an English teacher with the Peace Corps. After completing an exhausting and demanding twelve weeks of training in language as well as cross-cultural and technical skills, I felt more than adequately prepared for the challenge of teaching in an under-resourced school system designed on a colonial model.

Even as I entered the pastel pink building, I noticed a strange absence of noise, consideering it was the first day of school. A few isolated students wearing white school jackets rambled about in the dimly lit hallway. As I climbed the stairway to the administrative office, I heard a distant mango drop to the ground with a thud and a chorus of children's voices break out in glee. Hoping to catch a glimpse of the fastest one carrying off the ripe prize being pursued by the others, I looked out into the school yard and saw instead piles of old desk fragments, broken bricks, and tree branches. They must be cleaning the school grounds, I thought to myself. When I entered the office, the principal and his assistant were looking at a class schedule posted on the wall and discussing the large number of teachers that still needed to be hired by the Ministry. After greeting me warmly by inquiring about my health, my family back in America, and my life in general, they informed me that my teaching load had been increased by eight hours since the previous week. "No problem," I joyfully responded, "I love to teach."

The classroom where I was to teach was located a short walking distance behind the main building. Three lines of classrooms were arranged in rows much like military barracks. Since today was the first day of classes, I hopped on my bicycle and coasted right up to the door of classroom number 19—my classroom. "Always wiser to be punctual and prepared than be tardy and unequipped," I told myself. Two students were sitting inside the classroom playing cards when I entered. I looked at the official enrollment number of forty-seven and asked earnestly, "Where are the other forty-five students?" The card players faltered a bit and then mumbled, "They'll come, by and by." "Well, let's begin without them," I suggested, with a disapproving stare at the cards. They shrugged their shoulders and offered instead to go and find the students. It certainly didn't seem reasonable to me to teach two students and then have to teach the same material again when the others showed up later. Be flexible, I reminded myself, and so I agreed.

One week later, there were twenty-six students outside my classroom still waiting for the rest of their classmates to appear, by and by. I noticed that not only were students absent, but teachers as well. Meanwhile, the principal and his assistant were still discussing the schedule on the wall, moving multicolored pins, and deliberating how best to resolve the shortage of teachers. That morning I had stopped by the administrative office again just to make sure that I had understood correctly the radio announcement made by the Minister of Education the previous evening. I thought that he had announced that classes were in session and was quite relieved when the principal verified my assessment. He assured me that I had understood the Minister's announcement to the word and then asked me to teach an additional two hours a week. Lacking the experience to rebut his statement, "When there's a lack of teachers, we all need to pitch in a few extra hours," I nodded my head in consent. Considering that I wasn't actually teaching any students at the time, two extra hours didn't seem to be much of a burden, and I left, feeling only the slightest premonition that I might regret it later.

By the end of week three, I had managed to convince, cajole, and beg my students to enter the classroom. What other teachers did was their decision, I figured, but as for me, I was itching to do something other than wait on shore like a seafarer's wife. Once the students had entered, I discovered to my amazement that I couldn't get them to quiet down. Heedless of my requests to pay attention, they continued to socialize. Daisy painted her nails and chatted with Aminata about the new discotheque called Temptation that had just opened across from the mosque. Bebe took Nanda's notebook and wouldn't return it. Fatu gave me the peace sign and went outside to urinate. A few others followed. Students wandered in late with irrelevant excuses like "It's hot" or "I'm tired." Nelson and Marcelino held competitive jive talks while their classmates gathered around encouraging first one and then the other. Other students, whose teachers were absent, hung around the open windows, throwing crumpled up bits of paper to their friends. Others simply came to stare at me, a white woman who rode a bicycle to school. They shoved up against the outside wall, clambered over each other's backs, and stuck their heads in for a peek yelling, "White woman, white woman, there she is!" The next day, still more "window students" appeared to torment me. Such behavior continued daily and eventually I began to yell at them—"Get away from the windows!"—and resorted to pushing them out of viewing range. After one month at my new post, I reigned over thirty hours a week of complete disorder in a pseudo-classroom kingdom. This is madness, I thought.

For the next month, I devoted the first twenty minutes of class solely to establishing order and quiet. I was determined. I did this with gentle coaxes at first, but gradually evolved to using threats ("I'll call the school disciplinarian") and offering sweet enticement ("If you're good, I'll let you out early"). Late students were not allowed to enter, regardless of their excuses. It seemed the only way to control the chaos. Once I had my students' attention, I made them copy page after page of notes from the blackboard into their notebooks. I planned to inundate their minds with grammar rules and vocabulary lists so they wouldn't have time to talk. Other times, I made them repeat sentences in unison as if they were Berlitz parrots. Audio-lingual theorists suggest that language is acquired through repetition of recurring patterns, a proposition effectively demonstrated when I overheard my students mimicking me: "Be quiet! Go sit down!"

When the drudgery of memorization and repetition bored even me to death, I resorted to playing Bingo, Simon Says, or Do the Hokey-Pokey. I went to elaborate lengths to make nifty prizes for positive reinforcement and spent numerous hours designing creative educational posters to hang on the walls. For a time, I concentrated on visual stimulation and drama to reinforce right-brain learning, but the posters disappeared overnight and the drama idea erupted one day during a production of a local folk tale. I rather enjoyed their drama productions myself, and I figured they were reviewing English grammar and vocabulary by playing the games, but deep inside arose a persistent, nagging voice: "Surely, you can do more than baby-sit."

Gradually, as my disciplinary measures evolved to resemble boot camp philosophy, my classes began to develop a catatonic personality. Somber students stared back at me or out into space. Apathy replaced the boisterous noise I had become accustomed to combating. They refused to open their notebooks until I had repeated the request three times. Orders and instructions mollified them, sure enough, but now they didn't seem to have opinions, concerns, or even interests. Some simply put their heads down and slept. Sit and listen they did, but participate and discuss and collaborate they didn't. I wrote in letters to my friends back home that paper plates had more personality than these kids. Their passive resistance soon infuriated me, and I yelled in frustration at them, "I am here to help you. Don't you understand that?" They stared at me in a dazed disbelief. "What do you want?" I implored them with open hands: "Do you want me to entertain you? To treat you like military recruits? To punish you?" They shrugged their shoulders and sighed, "Teacher, we are pitiful. That's life." "Go," I told them. "Go home. Get out." They refused, of course.

Against my usually discerning judgment, I finally called in the school disciplinarian. The moment he arrived, every single student in the classroom jumped up on tiptoes to attention. They greeted him in perfect unison with a resounding "Good morning, Mr. Disciplinarian." When he ordered them to sit down, an immaculate silence spread throughout the classroom like a divine fog. I was astounded. They looked so serene and innocent as they waited attentively for his words. Their pristine, woeful eyes and composure made them appear as mere harmless babes, and I began to imagine that they would convince him of their purity and that I was the evil abuser. I began to wonder, in fact, if this wasn't perhaps partially true.

The disciplinarian picked out several students who were not wearing school jackets. In addition, he selected students who were wearing jackets, but had not buttoned the top button. He accused and convicted them of intent to belittle their American teacher and expelled them for two weeks, dismissing them with a disparaging comment. He then read a list of seven students' names. Since these students had registered for classes but had not yet paid their school fees, he expelled them for the year, adding yet another insult as they crept out of the classroom. He then turned to me and said, "If any one of these students ever gives you a problem, even the smallest problem, you tell me and I will expel the entire class for the entire year. Not one of them will pass, and they will all have to repeat the year next year." As I struggled to come up with an appropriate response to his comment, he turned back to the students, held up one finger, and challenged them, "Just one of you try it. Just one and I'll whip your ass." He left, but not before making an attempt to reassure me with a vindictive smile. I stood in horrified shock and embarrassment. I had just lost thirteen students. The students said nothing. They stared at me and waited to see what I would do next. I felt angry and stupid and offered a feeble apology. I fumed all the way home.

That night I dreaded ever going back into the classroom again. I contemplated terminating my Peace Corps service and going home. I was sure I could find a justifiable excuse to allow me a graceful exit. It was now the third month of teaching and quarterly grades were due in ten days. All I had managed to teach were two review units. Two review units! My God, I realized looking at their grades. Most of these students couldn't even meet the standards of the previous year's curriculum! How did they manage to pass? I was tempted to flunk them all myself this time around, but what would that accomplish? I looked in dismay at the stack of twenty-five lesson plans I had diligently prepared during the late night hours of the past two months and realized that I would never implement them.

So I switched strategies. That night I drew up a "No More" list. No more colorful visual aids to catch their attention. No more fancy vocabulary and grammar handouts for them to grab eagerly. No more games and no more prizes. No more school disciplinarian to resolve the ongo-

ing state of classroom crisis, either. My next unit began with
the following dialogue.

Teacher:	I am angry. I cannot teach because you do not respect me.
Students:	No, no, Teacher. Please, Teacher, please.
Teacher:	I don't want to teach you. I'm leaving.
Students:	No, Teacher, no. Please, Teacher. You see, you don't understand our situation.
Teacher:	Well, tell me, just what is your "situation"?

This time the dialogue was theirs to complete and resolve.

Her Students' Perspective

It was Tino and Mando who came and told us that a
skinny, sickly white woman had jumped off a bicycle, run
into our classroom, and tried to teach them English that
morning. Tino and Mando weren't even in our class: They
were just sitting there waiting to use the soccer field when
she rushed in like the rains. They weren't sure what to say
because she looked so strange. Her hair was all falling
down, and she wore a dress that looked like an old faded
bed covering that one might have bought from a
Mauritanian vendor in the used clothing market. We all
walked over to Nito's house and found a few more of our
classmates sitting out back drinking frothy tea. We decided,
even though school hadn't really started yet, that we'd go
the next day to see what this new American teacher looked
like. Tino and Mando assured us that she was as ugly as a
newly hatched, greedy-eyed vulture.

We knew that practically no one would be at school yet.
Most students were still on the farms finishing the harvest,
and others were still trying to register and pay their fees.

The Ministry had changed the admission rules again. All registrations completed at the end of the last year were now declared invalid, and so we had to wait in line, get new photographs, show our papers, and pay fees all over again—either that, or pay some official to put our names on the list, which actually was much easier than completing the registration process. We listened to the radio broadcasts by the Minister at night reminding parents of school and smiled. Everybody knew he sent his children, for good reasons, to the private, elite Portuguese School. Teachers at the public schools never showed up until the third week. Didn't she know that?

As it turned out, we agreed to enter the classroom just when everyone else did. We always say: "Cross the river in a crowd and the crocodile won't eat you." From that first day, she never demanded our respect. She didn't seem to care if we wore our school jackets or not. She didn't write the teaching summary on the board like our other teachers, and she was always in the classroom before the bell rang. That meant we could never stand up and honor her entrance. She should have known not to enter until after the bell rang. And she never took roll call first, as she should have, and so we continued chatting and doing our homework. Of course, by this time, other students had heard about our white woman teacher and were coming by to look at her and watch our class. We couldn't resist joining in the fun. At times, we believed she was serious, for example when she told the students outside class to leave. But where were they supposed to go? The area in front of her classroom was the designated student recreation area. Instead of ignoring them and us, she berated them with gestures and scolded us in Portuguese. Her Portuguese wasn't bad, but it sounded so amusing when she said "spoiled brats," you just had to laugh. We laughed even harder every time she said "Peace Corps" because in our Kriolu language "Peace Corps" sounds like "body of fish." We called her the "fish-body teacher" after that.

Classes were interesting because they were so confusing. She kept switching her methods, and we were never sure what to expect next. For a while she insisted that the mind equips itself and a teacher must not interfere in the process. She called it "The Silent Way." After the "The Silent Way" came "Total Physical Response." We gave actions to everything and pretended to be desks, pencils, and other classroom articles. We contorted our bodies into their defining characteristics and played "What am I?" Then we role-played imaginary dialogues between, for example, two books fighting to get into a book bag at the same time. One day she taught us the song "In the Jungle." We loved that song and still sing it after school when we walk home. No, you couldn't really call her a consistent person, but we all have our little ways. Even so, "a cracked calabash can still be mended." Obviously, she cared about us because she worked so hard to prepare for class. Most of our teachers were so busy at home or working a second or third job, they often missed class, and when they did show up, they never prepared anything. It's true that we've already learned more English this quarter than we learned all last year.

We always wanted to do more activities and play new games, but she seemed to think we needed to write. Because we didn't have books, she kept demanding that we copy information down on paper. But Guineans are oral people. We learn by talking; we make discoveries by sharing our experiences; and we help others by listening and contributing to conversations. Our history is a collective memory, and we are continually passing our knowledge on to others in our speech. She wanted us to raise our hands, one by one, and then talk individually. That to us seemed artificial and disruptive to the story-telling flow of human conversation. Only wolves howl individually.

She confused us even more by saying pointless things with vigor —"Wake up!" "Discover yourselves!"—or asking questions that had no obvious answers: "Why are you here?" or "What are you going to do?" Then she'd wait with such an intent expression on her face that we'd say almost anything to try to please her. We always enjoyed her facial expressions because they foretold what was soon to follow in speech—anger, joy, disappointment, praise, or contentment. She really should have learned by then how to hide and disclose her reactions in order to suit her goals more effectively, but she didn't seem to care. In some ways, she was just like a child.

We just didn't understand why it was our thinking that needed to change, and never hers. She wore a "bad eye" charm around her neck, so we thought she believed in superstition but when we asked her, she said she wore it not because she believed in superstition but to show respect and affirmation for our culture. We asked her if that was why foreigners always wanted to buy our ritual masks and initiation staffs, but she didn't respond. She told us we didn't need World Bank handouts and International Monetary Fund debts. What we needed, she said, was to learn how to grow fish. Was she crazy? We need computers, not fish! Balanta women always know where to find fish. "Teacher," we told her, "you will come and go, but we stay here." How could she understand our culture? She had only seen the rains fall once.

After a while, the novelty wore off, and we got tired of even a white woman's ways. It's hard—waking up at daybreak, doing morning chores, and then going to school for five hours without eating breakfast. Her class was during the last hour and we were as hungry as feral street cats by that time. Some of us lived far from school, and if our stepuncle or older cousin-brother told us to go to the market before school, we had no choice. We were forced to run to her class with only a bellyful of worms because we knew she wouldn't listen to our misfortunes even if we arrived two minutes late. It's true! In America, time is money, but here we don't respect time. Time is just now, nothing more.

It wasn't only that we had responsibilities at home that came before school—sometimes we were sick. If we had malaria, we'd put our heads down and sleep. And if we had "runny belly," we'd just run out of class when the cramping started. The dry season was so hot we faded away like morning song birds. One day she yelled at us. We admit, we weren't cooperating, but people are like that. We forgive each other and just go on. "That's life," we'd tell her. "A log as long as it stays in the water will never become a crocodile." Many things we just accepted as natural and impervious to change, but she considered such an attitude "fatalistic."

Finally, she called the school disciplinarian on us. She should have done that much earlier, in our opinion. We played our roles by allowing him to throw out a few students, because we all knew they'd be back as soon as he got some cashew wine money from them. Anyway, that's the right of elders in our culture, and we're taught in the bush school to abide by the established hierarchical roles. We didn't understand why she apologized after he left, and we couldn't believe it when she undermined his authority by apologizing for his "poisonous pedagogy," as she called it. Like a Guinean woman, she certainly had courage.

Today she did something different again. She came in and wrote a dialogue on the board. She asked questions about the dialogue that made us disagree. We had a lively discussion in English and then got into our groups and began designing some resolutions for the problem presented in the dialogue. We always say "When the ants unite their mouths, they can carry an elephant."

We know she'll stay, too. We saw it in her eyes.

Roz Wollmering (Guinea-Bissau, 1990-92) has an MA in Chinese from the University of Minnesota and a BA in Spanish and Biology from Saint Cloud State University, Minnesota. Writings about her Peace Corps experience in West Africa have appeared in *Violet Ink, The SHE Company*, and the Minnesota Women's Press.

Sierra Leone, West Africa

An Inconvenience Is an Adventure, Rightly Viewed

By Kinney Thiele

At dusk the first day upcountry—a day filled with colorful uniformed school children singing us into town, dancing masqueraders, speechmaking, and the moment I'd anticipated with the most hopes and fears, moving into the home of a local family—at dusk that day I learned how to take a bath. It wasn't a trivial exercise.

I'd returned from an introductory walk through town overcome with physical exhaustion and jet lag. Amadu, the youth who seemed to be in charge of me, immediately came to the door, however, carrying a pail. I took the hint, gathered a towel, cup, and soap from an overstuffed suitcase, and after self-consciously locking the door, willed my middle-aged body and overwhelmed mind to complete one more activity.

At fourteen, Amadu was gangly. He lugged the brimming bucket of water in one hand and motioned with the other to follow him to an enclosed area attached to the privy. In careful secondary school English he asked if I knew how to take an African bath. I hesitated at the unexpected question. He mimed: Fill cupped hands, splash, rub all over, splash. A smile flickered. "That," he said, "is African bath. All clean." He shrugged, turned abruptly, and took a few steps toward the house. There he sat on a ragged stump of a palm beside a spotted kid. She bleated and strained at her tether.

I grinned as I entered the stall gingerly. Rusty metal, supporting sticks, and sandy earth were all there was to see. No hooks. No bench nor shelves. The semblance of privacy was questionable. Through the lacework of decaying corrugated metal walls I could watch a half dozen children just a few feet away hacking open coconuts with a machete. A farmer ambled by with a lumpy, overstuffed bag balanced on his head and a hoe in his hand. I could hear him breathe. Amadu's mother, Isatu, had warmly welcomed me earlier that day. Now she bent over a supper fire near the back wall of their pink mud-brick house.

I stood a moment transfixed. After years of pausing before museum dioramas and dreaming of this day, Africa surrounded my curious eyes, animated, real. Despite humid heat, harsh conditions, and nervous fears I burst with the thrill of it all.

The latrine—a bath area and privy combined—was at the far edge of their clean, bare earthen yard near the border of dense brush. The privy was roofed. The bath stall remained open to the sky. Walls were built from recycled sheets of roofing tied or nailed onto raw sticks crusted with dry, flaking bark. Shaggy coconut and oil palm trees spread their fronds overhead. Underfoot the sandy ground was lightly graveled except where Amadu set the pail on a broken chunk of concrete.

The privy—a two-holer—was a walled concrete slab with small squat holes partitioned, one side for the family and one for me. Surprisingly, the area didn't stink. I noisily scraped aside the wooden cover with one foot and looked in. The pit was scary–ten feet or more deep.

I disrobed cautiously, trying not to drag my clothes in

the water or drop them, and strung them with the towel over the most eroded holes. An older boy crossed the yard to the well by the house and glanced at the enclosure. I felt intensely self-conscious. A brouhaha of ridiculous insecurities and cross-cultural questions battled good sense: They must be curious. Can they see in? Do they want to see in? Does it matter if they see in? Why do I care? It's so dumb to care. Take the bath.

I'd purchased a plastic cup in an open market on a training exercise the day before, though I never imagined its usefulness. Now I poured water over my sweat-soaked head. It flowed and meandered in sensuous, soothing rivulets down to my sandaled toes. I soaped up well and began to relax, continuing to watch the world around through the wall.

A pair of children nearby, poised like frogs, bounced forward and back, jousting. A skinny dog loped up to the fire where a pot, supported over coals by three stones, steamed. He flopped beside a tall wooden mortar tipped on its side that a youngster straddled. One dusty foot stretched out and shoved the mutt away.

Palms arched silhouettes against the deepening dusk and rustled in a sudden breeze. It was a storybook moment, until the soap shot out of my hand. It ricocheted off a wall and landed in the sand. I wiped it off as best I could. It rocketed off again.

Slowly I rinsed, toweled, and tried to put on a muumuu, but my body was still wet. I toweled more and observed stars beginning to twinkle through the atmospheric haze. I was still dripping. In fact sweat was pouring out faster than I could dry. My clothes stuck. As I wrestled them on I envied Isatu in her lappa, a length of cotton cloth easily wrapped and knotted into place by women of the tropics.

Equatorial nights fall fast. When I emerged, not all so long after starting, it was dark. The Southern Cross hung off to my left. Amadu picked himself off the stump, took the empty pail from my hand and led the way back to the tiny

pair of rooms I now called home. The giggling jousters had
vanished and the other children, now under the eaves,
barely glanced up. Mommy Isatu murmured *kushe* (hello)
as I passed her still at work over the smoky fire.

　　Of course no one had noticed or cared about the routine
event except me. It was a trivial activity. But it also became
a private baptism into life as it would be—public, complicated, and new, day after day. My desire to remember it all
deepened that evening. For 799 days I often looked back,
one gritty lesson after another, and thought, "If I'd gone
home last week I'd have missed...."

Kinney Thiele　(Sierra Leone 1985-87) was a health and rural development Volunteer in Taiama, Kori Chiefdom. There she worked with the
local professional staff to open an adult education center and take health
lessons to off-road villages. She holds an M.Ed. from the University of
Massachusetts/Amherst and works as the Inquiry Coordinator for SRI
International, a research and consulting firm in Menlo Park, California.

Micronesia, South Pacific

Everyone Everywhere Has Tales to Tell

by Carol Severance

One of the more extraordinary trips I experienced while a Peace Corps Volunteer in Micronesia was on the trading vessel *Maria Carmela*. I needed to travel from my home island of Ettal in the lower Mortlocks of Chuuk (formerly Truk) to the district center one hundred fifty miles away. The trip took five days.

Because Ettal had no pass into the lagoon, all loading of sea-going vessels took place via outrigger paddling canoes. We passengers and all of our gear bobbled up and down on the ocean swells as we waited to climb abroad the larger *Maria Carmela*. The climb itself was very awkward for those of us wearing skirts, the only acceptable dress for outer-island Chuukese women.

Aboard, the weathered deck of the *Carmela* trembled with each throb of her engine and the fetid odor of diesel fumes rode heavily on the humid, tropical air.

The captain pushed his way through the colorful crowd attempting to prepare his vessel for departure. He shouted orders to passengers and crew, and at last the visitors clambered over the side and back into their canoes. The engine rumbled louder, and we were on our way.

The deck of the hand-hewn *Carmela* was thirty-nine feet long. There were forty-eight men, women and children aboard as it traveled away from Ettal. There were also thirteen hens, a rooster, and a litter of pigs.

Freshly caught tuna hung from the mast and hundreds of green drinking coconuts filled the deck and wheelhouse. Even the engine room had its share.

When I asked if anyone had ever been lost overboard on a moonlit night, the captain glanced around the crowded deck, grinned, and said, "I have no idea."

The trip itself was filled with storytelling, singing, and laughter. I heard traditional tales of caution and wonder, and gossip unending about islanders from near and far.

Favorite among the stories were those about local Peace Corps Volunteers. Like the couple who had become so upset when the case of toilet paper they had ordered was lifted soaking wet from the bottom of the field-trip ship's hold. What could they possibly want with that big box of wet paper, my shipboard companions wanted to know.

There was one about a Peace Corps fellow from...well, never mind the island. He'd been caught dallying with a local girl behind the school house. I'd heard the story before, but the embellishments added during the *Carmela* retelling turned it hilarious. The islanders often competed with stories about their PCVs—who could speak the language best, who could sing, or sew, or paddle a small canoe without tipping it over.

I sat blushing through a tale of bravery I had unwittingly created when a sailing canoe on which I'd been a passenger had passed directly over two sleeping whales. Never mind that I didn't know at the time what the whales were and had thus hung curiously over the side to inspect them as we passed.

"If the whales had awakened, they would have played with the canoe," the storyteller assured his audience. "The whales wouldn't have hurt the people, but after they left, the sharks would have."

The story brought slowly shaking heads and many clicking tongues. Ettal was fortunate to have such a fearless American among them, the listeners agreed. Only a few grinned openly.

The weather remained calm and placid throughout the voyage, a blessing to the Chuukese women, who assured me they would otherwise have been quite seasick the entire way. For the same reason, I was more than happy to be sailing on a summer-smooth sea. Dolphins paced the *Carmela* from time to time, leaping and spinning, racing ahead, then dropping back to ride the bow wave. We saw giant sea turtles and schools of flying fish, but no whales. That resulted in another telling of my fearless whale adventure. I noticed a number of added details the second time around.

I was an artist when I entered the Peace Corps, and I took my paints and brushes so that I could document my stay. I hadn't counted on the ants eating the sealant off my carefully stretched canvases, or on the vivid tones of the tropics. My pallet included colors better suited to landscapes near my Colorado home.

So I began writing down the scenes I wished someday to paint—describing the giant breadfruit tree outside my house, the low sweep of green surrounding the pristine blue of Ettal Lagoon, the faces of laughing children.

In the meantime, I listened to the stories the islanders told. As my language skills grew, I began to recognize how they turned simple news into anecdotes to capture their listeners' interest, and when a story proved worth retelling, added more and more colorful details. In my journal, I began adding details, too—sounds and smells, tastes and textures. My tales grew more complex. By the time I left, my words provided a much clearer image of the islands than my paintings ever could.

I have continued to write since that time. I trained and worked as a journalist first, then returned to telling stories of the islands. Now I write novels and short stories and plays, based most frequently on Pacific Island lore and lifestyle. When I read from my first novel, *Reefsong,* on the University of Hawaii at Hilo campus, a group of Chuukese students came to listen. They grinned at recognized settings and events, and laughed freely at my island characters' foibles. I felt like I was back on the *Maria Carmela.*

I can still smell the diesel fumes and the thick pungency of fresh-roasted copra that rode with us on that trip. In fact, I can still hear the captain's panicked call on the last day when the steering chain suddenly jammed. We were just entering the Chuuk Lagoon and were in serious danger of going aground. There was a mad scramble as chickens and children and piglets and fish were passed from hand to hand to clear way for the search. A hat blew overboard and a crewman almost followed. He was caught by those standing near and pulled back aboard.

Finally a cry of success came, then a wave of relieved laughter. A coconut, the last of those piled abroad at Ettal, had become wedged tight against the open steering chain. It was yanked loose, and after a brief detour to rescue the lost hat, we were once again safely under way.

The story of that errant coconut was told many times during the following months. Each time it grew in excitement and tension. My Peace Corps experience taught me that the world is full of stories. Good or bad, sad or happy, everyone everywhere has tales to tell. The people of Chuuk tell some of the best.

Carol (Wilcox) Severance (Chuuk, Micronesia 1966-68) is the author of *Reefsong,* a science fiction novel describing a possible future for Pacific Islanders, based in part on her Peace Corps experience. *Reefsong* received the 1992 Compton Crook Award for best first novel. She is also the author of *Demon Drums, Storm Caller,* and *Sorcerous Sea,* a Pacific-oriented fantasy trilogy. She resides in Hilo, Hawaii with her husband, former Chuuk Volunteer Craig J. Severance.

Chile, Latin America

George Brett's Batting Average?

by Dwight Wilson

I entered Peace Corps/Chile over the July 4th holiday, a month after graduating from college. Almost all the trainees in our group were in their twenties, and most everyone must have been as wide-eyed and eager as I because one of the oldest trainees, a woman in her mid-thirties, nicknamed us the glowworms. We considered it a compliment.

One afternoon we visited an older man said to be one of Chile's most innovative horticulturists. A first look at his house confirmed the advance billing. Huge watermelons rested on the roof. Strawberries on beds of newspaper popped out of rusted fifty-five gallon drums. Every available inch of property seemed to be under cultivation.

Once inside, we seated ourselves around the host, who was in his late sixties or early seventies. He struck me as the quintessential creative genius, a rebel with much pride and probably few friends. In the middle of his speech, he paused, glared at us, and asked, "What do you know? And why are you here in Chile?"

One at a time, we tried to come up with sensible answers. Seth knew as little as I did about gardening but he could sling the bull pretty well, so I looked to him for some guidance. But Seth came up short, a bad sign. Even Jose, one of the few of us who really did know a lot about gardening, didn't sound too convincing.

I was getting more nervous and angry. "What do you know?" How dare he ask that! All I could think to say was that I knew George Brett's career batting average. But our host never called on me. Maybe he never saw me or maybe he could spot a wise guy from a distance. My line did get a laugh in the jeep on the way back to the training site, when some humor was still needed. We had left not long after the inquisition ended, the communal glow fading quickly.

What *did* I know? I wasn't sure. And then it came to me. I knew how to get along with people. I knew how to bring people together. No, I didn't know a great deal about gardening or almost anything technical for that matter, but I was sure I could bring together those who did with those who wanted to learn, or that I could do whatever it would take to reach an end result in a positive, empowering fashion.

That realization served me well for the next two and a half years in Chile and Honduras. It gave me the necessary shot of confidence to believe I could accomplish any project I set my mind to, however technically difficult. While I gained come technical skills and shared them, it was my "people skills" that accounted for whatever success my projects may have had. I brought people together and we worked in peace. I learned much about the frustrations and joys of cooperating with people who see the world in a very different, and equally valid, way.

What would I tell my friend outside Santiago today? I would tell him I know that our planet is desperately in need of greater cooperation, and that each of us has much of value to offer everyone else regardless of nationality, age, color, sex, or belief system. I would tell him I know that getting along with others, even making the effort to do so, can be tremendously difficult and satisfying. I would tell him I know deep in my heart that all of us—Chileans and Argentines, Hondurans and Nicaraguans, Russians and North Americans—can live and work in peace. I might even tell him George Brett's lifetime batting average, if I could remember it today.

Dwight Wilson (Chile/Honduras 1981-83) served as a rural community development specialist in the Peace Corps. He is the President of Cascadia Quest, a Seattle-based non-profit which brings together college-age men and women from around the world to carry out environmental restoration work in the northwestern U.S. and British Columbia.

Cameroon, West Africa

Development Is Down This Road

by Abigail Calkins

Few recognize me without my trademark Suzuki. Now I have this red Yamaha DT they gave me to replace it. I'm still white, though, or so they keep insisting as I pass by the shouting voices trying to get me to stop to do a favor, chat, or taste the latest in palm wine. I know I have a bike, but how do you say "I'm not a taxi" in the local language? I'm late, I'm in a hurry, I've got to help a women's group plant rows of plantains and pineapple in their community farm. This road could jostle my insides right out of me. My thighs are sore from being abused as nonstop shock absorbers. Yet nothing beats a forestial commute: a time to take in the bush meat hanging for sale along the way. Someone must have made the road longer today; all my landmarks keep reappearing. Didn't I pass that tree already? No, wait, here we go, time to cross the dreaded swamp. Water's high this morning, but I'm pretty sure I can make it through, feet up in the air, water splashing to the sides, engine roaring and...it dies. Shit! Is it possible to kick-start this thing without putting my feet down? I balance momentarily, contemplating the impossible. Reluctantly, I submerge my wonderful, quickly aging leather boots, feeling them flood, soaking my jeans up to my thighs. I dismount and push the bike grudgingly through the water to the other side. I hate this job, I hate this job, I hate this job. The bathers must wonder about the crazy white woman talking to herself. One little girl is crying because my yellow helmet makes me look like a monster. So I take it off. She starts shrieking. White people are ghosts. White people have funny hair and noses. White people who ride motos with helmets have strange markings of dust on their faces. Unable to pacify the kid, I shove on to the village, which is blissfully close. The president of the women's group is waiting for me. Sloshing over to her, I rip off my gloves and helmet to embrace her. At last, we can get down to business. Drums sound nearby. Uh oh...not drums! Not again! Not after this hour and a half drive! Not after crossing the dreaded swamp! The president leads me to a group of dancing women, who each hug me and invite me to join them in celebration of an old man who lies dead on a cot. We dance, and I try to conceal my discomfort in celebrating death, even that of an old man. No community farms today, folks. Development will have to wait. When the drums finally stop, the group escorts me somewhat officially to the president's house. They tell me they want to try making soap. This, after all, is the kind of technical know-how a white woman on a red motorcycle should have. Frankly, I don't have the first clue about soap-making. They unknowingly introduce me to the process: lye, blanched palm oil, and three hours of stirring. The women are singing songs, songs about soap, and my heart lifts as I help them stir. Someone brings me corn on the cob and warm beer. I look around. Such strength! These women with wide, open faces and old but colorful scarves wrapped around their hair, gossiping and laughing and occasionally arguing. I love this job, this job is great, I wouldn't miss this job for the world. You women are wonderful, every one of you; you make your own soap, so what if you won't work on your community farm? Soap classifies as development, doesn't it? Thunder rumbles in the distance. It is getting late. I say, "Would it bother you if I leave now; I need to return home," and they look bothered and tell me that I must stay until the soap is finished. I oblige helplessly, pushing thunder out of my mind. More singing, stirring, and bickering, but at last the women pour the thick green soap into the square wooden mold and I take out my camera to capture the triumph. (I will say back home, "And this was the day we made soap!") The group presents me with a gift, a splendid, singular egg, beautiful and simple. It is an egg that I will eat with joy. That is, if it makes it home intact. That is, if I make it home intact. Speaking my local language thank yous and good-byes, I return grimly to my red chariot. So we meet again, beast. The swamp provides no challenge this time since my socks and jeans are still damp. My fears rest more with the deep, black mass of clouds to my left. How fast do I have to drive to arrive home before the storm hits? If I go 264 kilo-meters an hour, I could be in my house in ten minutes. Chickens and children will fly. Cars will flip over behind me, and I will never even hear the fracas. This motor is loud; this yellow padded cage on my head, heavy. Please don't rain, please don't rain, please don't rain. The first drops splash on my nose, followed quickly by a torrential downpour, drenching me almost immediately, a cold and cruel wet seeping beneath my kidney belt, sparing nothing. Wasn't it supposed to be warm in Africa? Swearing through my chattering teeth, I am forced to continue since there is no house in sight. Why do I do this? Why? I laugh in my ridiculous misery. Finally, I pull into a village where a group of men grills corn on a small fire, and they invite me to warm myself by it until the rain subsides. It helps. I stare out at the storm and the road; all the carefree days I glided past this village on dry dirt and never even appreciated my good fortune. Ten kilometers remain between me and my house. Streams of muddy water flood the road, redefining it. Soon it will look like chocolate frosting. Back to the bike, the helmet, and the last drizzle of rain. Home is just around the next few bends.

Abigail Calkins (Cameroon 1987-90) was a community development Volunteer in Abong-Mbang, Cameroon, where she worked with women's groups in ten villages. She has an M.A. in Public Administration/ International Development from Columbia University and a B.A. in International Relations and French from Tufts University. Calkins is now a Program Officer at the Cooperative Housing Foundation (CHF), an international development non-profit that specializes in shelter assistance throughout the world.

Botswana, Southern Africa

Kalahari Desert: Sunset

by Christopher Conlon

The sun is slow. It settles
its burning cornea into
the womb of the earth

as camels, shadowed against a bath
of blood, shuffle across the fading eye
toward the kraal, and sleep,

and smoky birds begin their night songs
and insects, their soft
and various chitterings.

Heat, savage and blind,
slinks away, like an old dog
finding a place to lie down, die.

And when the slow eye closes last,
tinier eyes, silver and shining,
awaken: blood becomes balm;

and everywhere, slow darkness
is a phoenix; and cradle-pink clouds
are the skeletons of fish.

Christopher Conlon (Botswana 1988-90) worked as a secondary school English teacher in the Kalahari Desert of Botswana. Pieces from his manuscript *Hands of Rain: Poems About Africa* have appeared in *America, Negative Capability, Wind,* and other publications. He received the 1994 Peace Corps Experience Award from *RPCV Writers & Readers*.

Dominica, West Indies

Local Generosity "Nose" No Limits

By Penny O'Brien

A h, Callaloo!" The quality of the callaloo is the yard-stick by which some West Indians rate their islands. I learned this soon after my arrival in Dominica. Callaloo is a thick soup, made of dasheen, onions, carrots, coconut milk, and other exotic tropical delicacies. Thus challenged, I vowed to create some callaloo that would raise my status in the eyes of the women in my village.

Dasheen, the main ingredient, is a plant with large, heart-shaped leaves. The edible tuber that grows underground is four to five inches in diameter, and may be a foot long or even longer. I was told the vein in the dasheen leaf must be peeled out or the soup would be scratchy. And only the young, new, center dasheen leaves could be used. I had no problem finding a bundle of fresh leaves at the market on Saturday morning. Everyone in Dominica goes to the market on Saturday morning, to sell their food or to buy it— and, of course, to keep up with the latest news.

One evening after work, I was ready to try my cooking skills. I peeled the veins from the dasheen leaves. About a cup of chopped leaves was enough. The tuber has a rough, hairy outer surface that must be carved off before the vegetable can be diced. Mix a cup of diced dasheen with several cups of diced carrot, sliced onion, green banana, and chopped garlic. Place these ingredients in a heavy pot, cover them with water, and cook until they lose their identity.

Getting the food ready to cook took more time than I had anticipated, so I was glad to take a break when my neighbor, Medita, dropped in on her way home from church. We shared rum punch, discussed the fishermen's catch, then got around to what I was doing.

"I'm trying to make callaloo." I explained, and told her what I had done so far. I was chopping the dasheen when she came in. She was just in time to show me how to peel green bananas. Nothing is easy in the Caribbean. First, use either lime juice or cooking oil on your hands to avoid staining. Carefully slit the skin of the banana lengthwise on the outside curve. Cut the tips from both ends. Use your thumbnail as a wedge to separate the peel from the banana. I learned in my early school days that the purpose of skin is to protect what is inside. The fruit of these green bananas is well protected.

The bananas were finally peeled and were cooking gently with the vegetables in the iron kettle that rested on a coal pot, which I had borrowed from a neighbor. A coal pot is a charcoal burner that comes in a variety of sizes and shapes. Mine was round, about fifteen inches in diameter, and was insulated with three inches of fire brick. A wire rack several inches above the bottom held the charcoal pieces. Lighting the charcoal is another native skill that required practice— at least for me. The charcoal is not the uniform round black lumps we use in the United States; instead it looks like chunks of wood, except it is black and much lighter in weight.

Back to the bubbling, smooth callaloo.

"What do I do next?" I interrupted Medita's description

of family structure, how Sybar and Lista were brother and sister by their mother, but Gertrude and Lista were sisters by the same father. They all lived with their mother and their own children in a tiny, three-room house with a minimum of friction.

"Now it is time to put in the meat," Medita told me after she removed the cover, stirred the pot, and inspected the contents.

"I don't have any meat," I told her. Whereupon she laid down the knife she was holding, fished in her pocket and pulled out a small packet of what was once white, now gray butcher paper. She placed it on the counter and carefully opened it. "What's that?" I asked of the round, hard yellow something with two holes.

"It's pig snout," she told me proudly as she picked up a sharp knife and cut it in half. I didn't know what to say. I wasn't sure I wanted pig snout in my callaloo, but I knew she was sharing half her family's provisions with me. I mumbled some kind of comment that I didn't want to take away from her family, but she insisted. The pig snout was rinsed in the pan of water kept in the sink for rinsing everything and placed lovingly into the soup pot.

Medita yelled to one of the young boys running past the house to fetch a coconut. A few minutes later he was back, and with his machete made quick work of chopping the green husk from the shell and carving off the top so the coconut milk could be drained into the soup.

The proof of the pudding (or callaloo) is in the tasting. Guardedly, I took a sip. It was smooth and tasty, and it didn't even need salt.

Penny O'Brien (Dominica 1991-93) was a science resource development Volunteer working with teachers to develop new methods of teaching science. O'Brien has a M.A. in Early Childhood Education from the State University of New York at Binghamton, and a B.A. in Zoology from the University of Iowa. She is the author of *How to Select the Best Child Care Options for Your Employees*. She lives in Silver Spring, Maryland and co-edits a newsletter for Dominica RPCVSs.

Tunisia, North Africa

YSWF ... Living in an Arab World

by Lora Parisien

Tunisia is steeped in Islam. It is everywhere, in the language, food, daily practice. It is the very fabric of life. Because it is such a dominant force, it cannot be ignored—it just is. For the outsider (particularly if the outsider is female), understanding the nature of this force can be a lengthy, arduous process. Men and women in this country are born of a religion—way of life—that systematically segregates them: separate duties, separate expectations, separate schools, separate rules. There is so much underlying tension about what men and women should or should not be doing, it is no wonder that the mere presence of an outsider is like a big snag in the static social fabric.

No amount of cross-cultural training could have prepared me for day-to-day life in Tunisia. It is often said by Tunisia's corps of Volunteers, "It is not the physical challenge of living here that is so difficult; it is the mental and emotional challenge." All at once I was unprepared to graciously absorb the daily onslaught of propositions I received. In the beginning, I was not sure I would be able to withstand the comments. Depending on my mood, I was tremendously vocal or exceedingly demure. My glow-in-the-dark white skin, my green eyes, my clothing—though archly conservative—were indeed Western. My mere presence on the streets invited attention from males of all ages.

I was assigned to the capital, Tunis, a city more crowded than any I had ever known. With 1.6 million residents, Tunis's streets are a teeming mass of people. At first I didn't have the nerve to venture outside and explore my neighborhood. I would lie on my bed and stare at the cracked ceiling or the tree I had painted on my wall. I would stay motionless, listening to mopeds whir through the crowded streets of the *medina* (the traditional walled city) and the constant hammering of the brass smiths outside my window. Cocooned, safe from every possible intrusion, I tried to ignore my obvious lack of courage. When I walked to the Bourguiba Institute where I taught English, a thirty-minute commute, I wore my Walkman for protection. I found listening to the B52s humorous because the nonsensical music screened out the predictable barrage and put a smile on my face at the same time. Eventually, I abandoned the radio because I began to feel that perhaps it was culturally insensitive. Instead, I counted the number of times I was approached during that thirty-minute trek.

After about six months, something magical happened. I started to feel as if Tunis was my home. Somehow, somewhere along the way I began to win the war of stares and stopped letting the comments chip away at my personality. I stopped feeling as though every incident was a personal attack in a war waged solely against me. I discovered it was pointless to let these occurrences bother me. A Western woman is fair game and rules don't apply. These exceedingly annoying and overconfident flirtations were just attempts to capture my attention, and my interest. They were also completely harmless. In fact, I was far safer in Tunis than I was in Detroit.

I also enjoyed a powerful tool. I had learned Arabic.

Not only was I able to understand the solicitations, but I could respond in the most creative ways! "Now that's not very polite, is it?" Or my favorite, *"Rude bellick, Allah bish yhizz lsaanik."* (Be careful or God's gonna seize your tongue.) Believe it or not, that comment exacted shock and laughter from my would-be aggressors, who would then apologize profusely. In training, our instructors had counseled, "Learn the language, learn the language, learn the language." Arabic not only met my basic communication needs, it was my first line of defense.

Once the language barrier started to dissipate, I began to see past my own comfort zone and my eyes opened to a culture much bigger and far more fascinating than I. I began to put things in perspective. I relaxed and found Tunisia to be infinitely complicated and fascinating. I became absorbed in the culture. In *Beyond the Veil,* Fatima Merniss writes,

> The Islamic Veil originated in 18th century Samaria. It was worn by Samarian women to symbolize a woman's freedom—that she should not be assaulted because she is shielded by the veil. Without the veil, she is tempting the man to think about sex. With the veil she saves him from the opportunity to have bad thoughts.

In Tunisia, married women typically wear the *saf-sari* (veil) covering from head to toe. Unmarried women can choose to conform to this code or not. It is often viewed as being submissive not only to God but also to men. What most Western women fail to understand is the freedom offered by a veil. Donning the shapeless sheet does not convey that women are not equal. A woman who chooses to veil is a woman who is convinced by Allah's word as it is written in the *Quran,* the holy book of Islam. It extends the idea of protectionism by secluding her in the holy world of Islam. She is *not* to be bothered. She is *not* fair game. She has made a conscious decision. Younger women in Tunisia are veiling. This, for the most part, is political in support of fundamentalism. There are some, though, that feel early the pangs of Islam. I had a Tunisian family who "adopted" me. There were three sisters. One, Besma, was my closest friend. She was free spirited and rejected the veil. Her sisters, ages fifteen and twenty-two, were very devoted to Islam...and very veiled. They even refused to let me see their hair (though they boasted that it was far more beautiful than mine) because I was not a Muslim.

The two sisters had chosen a different path—one that could never allow them to be sympathetic or understanding of Besma's free spirit. They were once like her, child-like, open, and far less serious. Along with the veil came a cloud that blotted out the memories of those days. Because Besma refused to veil, they could neither comprehend their middle sibling nor tolerate her. Besma was not rejecting the presence of Allah in her life. She was expressing her desire to have an identity, not hide it. Long walks, arm in arm, through the crowded alleyways of our jam-packed neighborhood put the daily struggles of life in perspective for both of us and gave us respite from our more serious sisters.

One evening, very late, there was a knock at my door. It was rapid and continuous.

I yelled, "*Shkoon?*" (Who is it?)

"Besma," came the reply. "*Fsa, fisa.*" (Hurry up.) I opened the door. "You must come over to my house right now, please."

"What's wrong?"

"My mother wants to see you and dinner is waiting."

Although it was late, I was accustomed to these impromptu invitations to meals at the Tounsi household. I changed out of my shorts and t-shirt and into an ankle-length skirt and loose, flowing shirt. We walked hurriedly through the narrow streets, in and out of the complicated labyrinth of the medina to her neighborhood. We knocked on her door in the same manner and heard her mother say, "*Shkoon?*"

"Besma and Noora." (Noora was my Tunisian name.)

The door opened and I was flooded with kisses by Besma's mother, Laila. She seemed especially excited to see me. She held my hand and escorted me through the courtyard into the family living area.

Upon entering the tiny chamber that served as a dining room, recreation area, and bedroom, the roomful of waiting people stood up to welcome me. Each came up to me, one by one, and planted the customary four kisses—two per cheek—on my face. I recognized almost everyone in the room as family and cousins. The only person not to greet me was an older gentleman who did not move from his seat but fixed his stare on me from the moment I came in the room. He seemed amused. Besma's mother once again grabbed my hand and led me to the couch, never releasing my fingers from her tight grip. I was seated facing the stranger and the room became very quiet.

Then the stranger started to speak. In perfect English, with a strong Arabic accent, he introduced himself as Uncle Mohammed. He gave me an abbreviated life story. He told me he was educated and that he "took" a degree in dentistry. He was financially secure and could promise me frequent vacations in Europe and a yearly trip to America to see my family. He explained that he had seen a picture of me—one that I had given to Besma. He knew the moment he saw it that I should be his wife. And...did I accept?

Dumbfounded beyond words, I looked around the room. Everyone was perched on the edges of their chairs. Except for Mohammed and me, no one in the room could understand English, so they were anxiously awaiting my re-action. I shot Besma a "what-have-you-done-to-me" look. When I turned to Laila, who had now deprived my fingers of blood flow for nearly ten minutes, she was frantically nodding her head yes, yes, yes! I looked back at Mohammed, who was waiting for my favorable reply.

"How old are you?" I asked.

"Forty-six," he replied.

"Wow," was all I could say.

"It's a wonderful opportunity for you," he said. "Really, the chance of a lifetime." Then Laila chimed in. "You will be in our family. I am so happy." She was already congratulating me.

"Besma, can I speak with you a moment?" I asked. Besma followed me into the courtyard.

"Really, Besma. He is only four years younger than my father. Too old for me, way too old. Could *you* marry someone twice your age?"

"No. I'm sorry. Everyone thinks it is such a perfect arrangement. You're alone here. What was I going to say? Don't worry. I thought you might not want to. Tell him it's impossible." Great. How was I going to gracefully decline without offending my Tunisian family? In their eyes it was as though Mohammed had handed me the keys to a brand new Ferrari and said, "Here, take it, it's yours." Who would say no to such an offer? We returned to the room. Everyone was prepared to jump right out of their chairs. I sat across from Mohammed.

"I am sorry I cannot accept your gracious offer. My family wants me to marry a man from my hometown, one I have known since childhood." It was a blatant lie. "He is waiting for my return. I am here because there is so much yet to learn. I want to be ready for marriage and right now I am not. I am too young. But when I am ready, it will have to be him I marry."

"I understand," he replied. "Thank you."

With that he got up and exited the room. Laila stared at me with puppy dog eyes and everyone in the room fell back into their chairs, defeated. Besma later explained my reasons. My Tunisian family seemed to accept them without question. Besma and I relived this encounter for weeks.

I was very comfortable being American—in America.

There were a million things that I never took for granted—
like my daily jog. Running was like eating breakfast, something I did everyday. Wearing shorts or spandex was just as
normal as wearing my favorite pair of perfectly broken-in
Nikes. So, when it occurred to me that I might not be able
to maintain this practice, I got a bit belligerent. In Tunisia,
running is something that is done on the soccer field, by
men. I went to great lengths to compromise, refusing to give
up my God-given right to run. But I needed to take precau-
tions not to bring undue attention to myself or embarrassment to other Volunteers.

My first attempts at running started during training in
Hergla, a tiny Mediterranean village. In order to avoid the
peculiar stares of Tunisians, I woke up at 5 a.m., pulled on
heavy sweats (though the temperature was already in the
high nineties) and clambered onto the road heading straight
out of town. The only creatures awake at that hour were the
wild dogs, which I had to fend off with large rocks. In
Tunis, I quickly tired of jogging in place in my bedroom.
Certainly racing around the streets of the capital was out of
the question. For a while, I caught the 6 a.m. Metro to Sidi
Olympique, a forty-minute ride. The bright turquoise
sweats under my skirt occasioned a stare or two. Once in
Sidi Olympique, I hid my skirt in a tree while I ran the trails
around the stadium. During my second year, I moved to the
country. I ran at the girls' school until the teachers required
their students to run *with* me. It wasn't long before the girls
resented my presence because it signaled an hour-long run
in the hot, early morning sun. So I adjusted my schedule to
run in the late afternoon. That didn't last either. My landlord
asked me to stop because I was becoming a spectacle and
the local men were gathering outside the school walls to spy
on me. Apparently I was more exciting than the karate flick
at the local cinema. I finally found one of my students who
was willing to run with me along the highway outside
town—as long as I taught her English along the way.

I feel very fortunate to have served in an Islamic country. Two years couldn't possibly have afforded me the time needed to fully grasp the complexity of this rich and mysterious culture. It happened to me, and I watched it happen to my fellow Volunteers—curiosity caught us. We struggled not to escape but to reach an understanding. Through our work, our friendships, our mere presence, we forged an understanding of ourselves and our hosts.

Lora Parisien (Tunisia 1989-91) was an English teacher at the Bourguiba Institute for Modern Languages-University of Tunis. She spent her first year teaching in the capital city, Tunis, and her second in the western city of Beja. Parisien has a B.A. in journalism from Central Michigan University.

Poland, Eastern Europe

Letter From Poland

by Mary Melinda Ziemer

In Poland, the distance is between events, not things, and I move in flux between World War II, the Gdansk shipyard strikes, and the new-world-order capitalists hawking goods. Ideally, part of my work as a Peace Corps Volunteer is to learn what it means to be Polish. After having lived in Poland for a year and a half, I've learned to look through the problems here to find the values that sustain the hope of this country.

Perhaps because of the war experience and the struggles of the past forty years, Polish people seem to be sensitive to life's tenuousness and its singular beauty. As a result, they've developed the gift of communion, stretching a social gathering into an all-day, sometimes all-night, affair. With miracle-of-the-loaves hands, they transform a few slices of bread, cheese, and tomato into a feast.

Underlying the loud and eager conversation of family and friends is the same quiet sincerity and thankfulness that I have noticed surrounding the celebrations of the Eucharist in Polish churches. Fortunately, my work as a teacher trainer has brought me into the private realm of Poland where people help one another to overcome the inefficiencies, frustrations, and insecurities of everyday life.

In the district where I live, the unemployment rate has reached thirteen percent, which means a good number of the people I sit with on the bus are probably out of a job.

Now, whenever I get together with my Polish host family or with Polish friends, the talk turns towards enterprise. When I miss the leisurely conversations of a year and a half ago, I have to remind myself that their talk is a matter of strategy and survival, not manners. At least four new language schools have opened in Torn, offering immediate success and wealth if a person will only sign up for English courses. Although such a claim is exaggerated, it reflects the need people have to learn a language that will enable them to understand the "rules" the West lives by. Business booms at these private schools.

At any rate, I teach English with the general philosophy that people use language to shape reality, to create a world view, an understanding of the human condition. Metaphorically, until a person learns to use his or her own language effectively he or she lives in a "developing country."

In Poland such abstractions take on concrete form. Vaclav Havel testifies to this in a speech he gave called "Words," where he explains "in the part of the world I inhabit the word Solidarity was capable of shaking an entire bloc." Poland, however, is a "developing country," not only because that which connects a modern society—banking, communication, and distribution systems, for example—is often disconnected or defunct, but also because Poland is undergoing what Timothy Garton Ash, a specialist on Eastern Europe, calls a "reconstitution of civil society." All the way from glee clubs to the government, Poland is in the process of redefining itself in a painfully literal way.

In the opinion section of the *Warsaw Voice,* a senior assistant at the National Museum, Alfred Twardecki, claimed that "conceptual chaos reigns in Poland." In his view, Polish society needs the ordering power of clearly defined words: "defining what is meant by a democratic system, and starting a public discussion on the fundamental principles on which Poles want to construct." That, he wrote, is essential if Poland is to have a stable society and government.

While Poles reconstitute their society, it is my hope that my students can use their English language skills to keep traditional Polish values, the emotional, intellectual, and spiritual life of the people, from being "deconstructed" by the jargon and jingoism of consumerism. One of my students recently told me that she had studied English only as a means to emigrate because she could see no future for herself in Poland. But after a year of study at the Teacher Training College, she had determined to stay in Poland and make her living as an English teacher. She is the "advance guard" that will give form to Poland's national determination, and I am honored to have been a part of her training.

Mary Melina Ziemer (Poland 1990-93) was a teacher trainer at a teacher training college in Turun, Poland where she coordinated a three-year English language program. Ziemer has a M.A. in English from California State University Fullerton and now lives in Leysin, Switzerland.

Nigeria, West Africa

Shakespeare in Calabar

by Tom Hebert

This old postcard still hangs there in my mind: a
King—The Muri of Ifut—his several courtiers, and
the several wives of the Obong of Calabar, all bunched
against the wild rain, the Guinean tempest howling up from
the Bight of Biafra, a love-besotted Irish Holy Ghost Father
clinging to the weakening Inner Above, passing a South
African exile a fifth of Vat 69 ("All the better to hang on to
that upright with"), while a full-sized Elizabethan stage
sank slowly into the turf of a West Africa soccer stadium.
Right then I hoped that it wouldn't ever get much better because a person can withstand only so much fulfillment in his
life.

Sunk deep in the slack creeks that slowly wash out to
the Atlantic, in 1964 Calabar was still a Victorian, Sadie
Thompson kind of place. This crinoline tramp had, for generations, been compromised beyond redemption by her ap-
petite for the British district headquarters and her earlier
partnership with the slave factors' hulks that had stained her
dark waters. But Calabar town, before Nigeria's recent oil

boom and bust, had style, panache, many terrific secondary
schools, and boasted numerous living relics from her colonial time: literary societies, bookstores, Pim's Cup #2,
snooker at the club, formal balls and her flat-out four-
wheel-drive love for Shakespeare.

My Peace Corps assignment was so perfect I hesitate to
talk about it even now, fearing that someone will yet take it
away. After one in-country year of teaching high school
English, I wangled an appointment as business manager for
the School of Drama at the federal University of Ibadan (the
first Volunteer accepted there since the famous Michelmore
postcard incident). For the School's first Theater-On-
Wheels cross-country tour, I was named the advance man,
traveling around the country creating local civic committees to handle promotion and logistical arrangements for the
upcoming 3,000-mile tour.

That year, celebrating Shakespeare's 400th birthday,
we presented an evening of four hours of scenes from his
plays. A truly lavish production, it rolled through the country on a forty-foot truck-trailer combination that at each of
the twenty-three host towns opened up into a stage, like a
huge plywood sunflower. All funded by Shell Oil, the
British Council, and the Ford and Rockefeller foundations,
there was a bus for the forty student actors, four staff cars,
and the advance man in a circus-painted Land Rover hung
with loudspeakers, flinging gaudy flyers to a million town-
folk. A sensational juggernaut highballing it from savannah
to coastal delta, to Sahel and back.

Astonishingly, in the West Africa of this period lay the
most Shakespeare-literate society the world has known
since sixteenth century London. Secondary schools in
Nigeria, Ghana, The Gambia, Sierra Leone, and Cameroon
still competed under the Cambridge University/West
African School Certificate Council's examination program.
The School Cert mandated, among other standards, that students study five years of Shakespeare to prepare for the final
examination's "set play." As a result, for several generations

millions of West African kids quite literally memorized two or three of William Shakespeare's plays. (Such heroic learning was much inspired by every Nigerian's lovely use of language and the daily reality of a national life then singularly Elizabethan in the epic grandeur of its debates and tribal intrigues of power and vivid character.) At our performances thousands would mouth the lines in an audible susurrus that confounds me now as I worry over what went wrong with American schools.

On my advance trip, learning that the patronage of Calabar's two Efik kings was necessary if the presentation was to happen, I had negotiated several details with their Royal Highnesses, the Muri of Ifut and the Obong of Calabar, and had come to know and greatly respect them. They immediately sent out the proper assurances and promised to be in attendance.

A month later, on the night in question, knowing we had presold 3,000 tickets, I asked my entire committee to be available for rough duty. At earlier stops we had had crowd scenes that bordered on riots, with a rush of 10,000 people pressing through the single stadium gate in Onitsha, kids hanging from telephone poles in Umuahia.

The backstage crowd that night included the priest who was vice-principal from St. Patrick's Secondary School, who, we all knew, was innocently smitten with a Calabar Volunteer (he would later suffer much more during the Biafran War from federal persecutors); a wonderful South African, teaching out his exile years in another local high school; the drama school's roguish English director; and several staff.

With an urbane Calabar audience seated without incident and the royals in their box seats, the lights came up on a ravishing *Twelfth Night*. But we were now hitting the rainy season. Two hours later, just after the scenes from *Julius Caesar* began, all hell broke loose. First the wind, then a small rain, then West Africa Wins Again! The speaker and light towers, rigged on cement-filled wheels, began to weave, while under the force of the wind the stage was coming unhinged. Soon the rain was blowing dead level across the footlights. Surely the audience would flee, but looking out we saw them rooted to their chairs. Electrical lines were arcing. Someone said that something had to be done. Perhaps the crowd wasn't leaving because the two royal parties hadn't budged. Detailed for the job, I scampered across the field to the royal enclosure. Crouching down by his armchair, I inquired of the Obong of Calabar, the senior of the two rulers, if he didn't think it best to call the whole thing off, so his people could find some cover.

His ear cupped to catch the now unamplified words, he looked up, smiled: "Thank you. I can't leave just yet. I haven't had time to read *Julius Caesar* in so many years. I don't remember now how it all resulted. And I, of course, should know. Remember, how 'Uneasy lies the head that wears the crown.'"

The next morning a heavy-duty tractor was engaged to unstick the stage from the field. The performance had, of course, carried on in the rain to a full, happy stadium. Calabar was my kind of town.

Tom Hebert (Nigeria 1962-64) is the co-author with John Coyne, of three books about innovative American training and education. He is currently writing a book entitled, *American Mavericks:Getting the Job Done, Changing the Way Things Are, Seeking the Greater Good.* He lives in Seattle, Washington.

Ethiopia, Horn of Africa

The Song Of Our People

by David Arnold

Addis Ababa, the capital of Ethiopia, is a quiet, broken city in the forested mountains of Africa, a city inhabited by 1 to 2 million refugees of political movements—royalists and communists—and by another million poor, crippled, and homeless who offer pity to one another on cobbled sidewalks.

Ethiopia is a geologic uplift on the Horn of Africa at the mouth of the Rift Valley. It rose as a Semitic culture imposed on African tribes, a medieval European city-state isolated in sub-Saharan mountains. As Ethiopian histories tell it, Addis Ababa became the nation's capital when the emperor's wife discovered hot springs during a royal afternoon picnic. Her husband, Menelik, pleased with her discovery, decided to move the palace in 1890 to the flank of a mountain at the northern end of the Rift Valley. Along with the king and queen came everyone else. It was a very Ethiopian thing to do during those feudal times.

Occasionally Ethiopia's feudal pageant caught the modern world's attention. There was His Imperial Majesty

Haile Selassie, trim bearded and of military bearing yet small in stature, pleading in the gloomy light of a dais at the League of Nations, or standing in the long shadow of General Charles DeGaulle at John F. Kennedy's funeral. Haile Selassie was the last of 200 kings and queens who claimed descent from King Solomon. The long lineage collapsed as the liberating spirit of the 1960s reached Addis Ababa. But the spirit passed on and for the following seventeen years, there was socialism and bloody terror. People here called it Derg's Time, for the governing committees (*dergs*) set up by the dictator General Mengistu Hailemariam. Following still another liberation in 1991 Ethiopia now plans another rebirth.

I have another Ethiopia in mind. A countryside where my wife and I lived for two years in a hillside house with blue wooden shutters and blue wooden doors. Out of open front doors, through eucalyptus branches and over the roof of the schoolhouse, we could see across the valley to an Orthodox church with ostrich eggs impaled on the three wooden points of its rugged Axumite cross. The sun rose behind the church each morning with clarity, slipping down the wooded side of Jello Mountain where some wildlife experts believed the rare mountain nyala lived.

At night, we graded papers under a flaring Aeroplane lantern. Next door a shepherd blew his bamboo flute over the crackling of the fire that blazed on his floor. Over the whooping of scavenging hyenas that skulked in dark streets, farm boys in smoky, circular huts drummed on goatskins. Their song filled the dark, cool nights of the Harar Province mountains.

Last year, for the first time since I was a Peace Corps Volunteer in the mid-sixties, I returned and heard their song as an Ethiopian friend and I walked through the Mercato district of Addis Ababa. The members of a roving band of Moslem pilgrims—snag-toothed men and turbaned boys— sat facing one another in a circle of drums, clothing, bundles of goods, and feet, chanting in the language of the

Oromo. The song they sang was one I remembered without knowing the words. It lifted me from Addis, like the repeating rhythms of the night train, jolting along the narrow-gauge tracks of the desert floor. I used to spend much of the thirteen-hour ride to our town hanging out the open second-class door holding onto the outside rail, bathed in the cold, black night of the desert, the jaundiced light of the cars blurring the African bush, the carved rock faces, the shrill peal of the deeper night when the cars crossed dry ravines.

When my friend, who is now a lawyer, was twelve or thirteen, he came to our house after school and wanted to learn everything. He had a broad smile that opened our hearts. He maintained the reserved nature of Ethiopians, but invaded our conversations with questions about refrigerators, the origin of freckles, and boxer Muhammad Ali. We exchanged details of our cultures. He told my wife and me folk stories from his, and quoted pithy wisdoms from the school's small library of ragged, out-of-print books. In the land of the blind, he once said, the one-eyed man is king.

When we left Ethiopia, our friend wanted to come with us. But we encouraged him to stay in Ethiopia and serve his country. Bright and eager to please, he scored well on eighth-grade leaving exams and received a scholarship to attend General Wingate School, a private secondary school operated by British teachers. He went on to Haile Selassie I University to study law. On the campus he joined antigovernment protests that led to the fall of Haile Selassie.

My friend didn't benefit from seventeen years of socialism. He desperately wanted to change his society, but he refused to join the Communist party. He studied the craft of survival as his nation fell apart in white and red terror campaigns.

He was employed by a succession of government agencies and became a sober, hard-working bureaucrat. When foreign governments came to negotiate trade and manufacturing agreements with the government corporations the lawyer represented, they took him to dinner at a local hotel.

Where did you go to university? they asked. Addis Ababa, he replied. Where did you go to learn to speak such good English? Right here in Ethiopia, he said proudly, smoothing his r's and flattening the a's of his Midwestern American accent.

During my recent visit, we took a series of taxi rides west of Addis, past the national leprosarium to a recreation park beside Meta Brewery. On the road, the lawyer pointed out a subdivision of houses Ethiopians describe as California style. The neighborhood is near an international high school run by Americans, and the center of the American military, development, and diplomatic community. My friend used to work as a gardener and grader of student papers for the school superintendent, and took the superintendent's daughters to American movies. But on the Haile Selassie University campus, he was a political activist and a leader in the student Marxist movement.

On a day two decades later, we were facing one another in the back of the blue pickup taxi in the socialist tradition of confrontation and dialogue. The lawyer offered to me what sounded like a confessional.

"We shouted for the Yankees to go home. They went home and we had nothing."

As we traveled together, the lawyer began drawing for me a small circle around his Ethiopian history. We would watch the evening news about the former Derg officers who were in prison waiting for war crime trials. "We were classmates," he said of one former ideologue. "We were Wingaters together." He also remembers friends from the eighth grade who are dead or in exile. Others, former friends, are now running the country. It is a small, dysfunctional network from which he has removed himself to survive.

Among family photographs and certificates on the wall of his home, the lawyer tacked a piece of paper on which he wrote, "This too shall pass." He is a bachelor approaching middle age and he lives in a small government rental duplex across the street from a former training center where he was once a prisoner.

In Derg's Time, the Ethiopian Orthodox Church was publicly ignored by the government. Soldiers piled stones in a wall from curb to curb to block the front entrance to Trinity Cathedral. But the stones did not discourage the devout. For many years believers entered the church through the graveyard in back of the church, climbing the hill in the chill morning.

While living in Ethiopia this time, I stayed in a house with a splendid view of Trinity Cathedral. The church is surrounded by a tall grove of eucalyptus. The dome appears wrapped in branches and the rows of sculpted saints who guard the dome are lost in the leaves. But the tall, naked trunks of the trees revealed the cemetery, where each Sunday morning Ethiopians dressed in traditional white cotton garments drift like spirits among the large, cradle-shaped gravestones of the churchyard.

"There is no other country in the world in which there are so many churches as in Abyssinia," wrote James Bruce of Kinnaird, a Scot who looked for the source of the Nile for seven years in the 1800s.

Once I followed a German tourist into an Ethiopian Christian landmark, Debre Berhan Selassie, a small 300-year-old church in Gondar. The church walls and ceiling are sealed with rich, graphic frescoes of Ethiopian and Christian history. The government guide, Teara, pointed to the figure of Abuna Tekle Haimenot. "He had one artificial leg because he stood reading the bible for seven years without stopping," the good-natured Oromo told us.

"It does not take seven years to read the Bible," the German said.

"Oh, but we have many, many bibles," Teara explained.

Angels surround the doorways. Their faces stand in rows on the ceilings, their ears like wings, and they stare down with large infant's eyes etched in black kohl. A monk named Abbe Hailemeskel painted the interior of this small

Sistine Chapel.

"It took him nine years," Teara told us. I pictured the priest prone on a scaffold, his arms aching with pain as he colored the black kohl that surrounded the angels' eyes. He gathered the colors for his paintings from the rocks, soil, and plants that surrounded the city, and from the blood of animals.

Easter in Ethiopia is like Christmas elsewhere. It is the high season that follows two months of fasting. On the day before Easter, I rode by taxi to the National Theater to see an Amharic production of the Greek tragedy *Oedipus*. Flocks of sheep stood in the gray mist along the roadside like Christmas trees in a Lions Club parking lot. The heads of several slaughtered cows had been discarded in the median of one boulevard, and municipal garbage bins were overflowing with the entrails of freshly slaughtered animals.

Abate Makuria, the director of *Oedipus*, rushed across the cold, care-worn National Theater before the Saturday matinee. He is one of the nation's popular dramatists, a small, round man dressed in fashionable running clothes, deck shoes and a floral print sports shirt. In a flush of energy, he waved to arriving members of his cast and offered an aside.

He wanted to show Ethiopia's tragedy to her people. Abate chose this Greek tragedy to perform, and staged it in the language and dress of modern-day Ethiopia, and set it in the beggar's place in the cemetery behind the churchyard.

I sat a few aisles in front of the loge where the royal family used to sit for private performances. Their faded velvet curtain was drawn shut, and before it stood actors dressed in the robes and crowns of priests. Their acolytes held massive silver crosses, struck small cymbals, and swung burners of incense, casting the sweetened smoke throughout the theater.

Then, as they walked down the aisle, they droned the priests' liturgy in the ancient Ge'ez language. In the wings of the stage—men on one side, women on the other—actors dressed as beggars huddled among wooden risers. The play was performed according to the Greek script, but the beggars and the priests held a mirror to their Ethiopian audience. I recognized the gross similarities between the drama of the state and the street outside.

On the following day, Abate stood at my living room window and talked about Oedipus in Ethiopia, smoking a series of cigarettes and pacing the carpet.

"This is a classical opera. The chorus was like a still life. The poor stoically played the chorus to the tragedies of its rules. Take Oedipus and Haile Selassie. Imagine. The people faced hunger, the people faced drought. The same situation. They appealed to him. 'Get concerned with the people,' they said. He didn't. He was concerned with himself. And when he realized, it was too late. It was just like Oedipus.

"The Derg didn't understand the values of the Ethiopian people. 'I will make a new man of you,' they said. It was an artificial gesture. The traditions are in my countrymen. It's an attitude, a vision. That's where the Derg went wrong. Communism didn't penetrate."

What inspired him to do *Oedipus* was the richness of the Amharic language. "You can say anything in the power of its poetry," said the director. "It is a song of our people."

David Arnold (Ethiopia 1964-66) is editor of *WorldView*, the quarterly magazine of the National Peace Corps Association. He worked on the staffs of three U.S. daily newspapers, wrote for several national magazines, taught journalism at several U.S. universities and was a Fulbright lecturer in Pakistan and Kenya. He holds a B.A. in English literature from Washington University in St. Louis, an M.A. in journalism from the University of Missouri at Columbia.

Peru, South America

Life On The Death Beat

by Ron Arias

Icover death. Whether it's in El Salvador, Ethiopia, Mexico, Nicaragua or Haiti, I report on what's left after the shooting, after the earthquakes, after whatever death leaves me. I've never thought of it as a ghoulish beat, especially since I write for *People* magazine. No, I'm just attracted to stories of aftermath—heroic, sometimes terribly sad, stories of human survival.

But I got a surprise one morning when my New York editor told me to fly to Los Angeles and interview five Costa Rican fishermen who had just survived five months adrift in the Pacific.

Finally, I thought, a story of real life on the death beat—a wonderful, sweet, triumphant life against tremendous odds.

I met the five Costa Ricans at the Los Angeles airport. The Ticos, as people from Costa Rica are known, had been rescued three days before by a Japanese fishing vessel seven hundred miles south of Hawaii. They were flown to Los Angeles for a brief layover on their way to Costa Rica.

None of them spoke English, so when I walked in and introduced myself in Spanish, it was as if they were welcoming a brother. *Abrazos* all around.

For the next few weeks, in Los Angeles and then in their barrio near the Pacific port of Puntarenas, Costa Rica, I soaked myself in the sea saga of the five survivors.

In late January 1988, a tremendous windstorm, locally called *ae norte,* wrecked their fishing boat; when the storm subsided, and their survival odyssey began in earnest. Near rescues, starvation, thirst, a makeshift sail, shark attacks, an island sighted, the friendship of a giant sperm whale, fights, arguments, a mutiny, and hellish bouts of desperation—all these events and more, I discovered, were the stuff of their fascinating true-life adventure. More than that, it was a story about the limits of human endurance, the deep bonds that hold people together.

To be able to narrate their story in their simple, straightforward manner, I cannot overemphasize my own lifetime preparation as someone who's never really left his Latino roots. I'm not just referring to my upbringing in a Mexican family in El Paso and Los Angeles.

It also has to do with my Peace Corps stint among the working poor in Peru. Everything that I've written with any depth and compassion has its roots in that period.

My partner and I lived in a valley south of Cuzco, helping feed kids in village schools, trying to raise rabbits and hogs, and—our showcase project—starting a cattle-breeding center with a pair of government-loaned Brown Swiss bulls.

They were big, beautiful animals, one fully mature, the other still an adolescent. On opening day, families from miles around came to watch, curious about how such beasts would perform with their puny local breed of cows.

But the young bull wanted to suckle udders, while his older partner was only interested in mounting him. It was a small lesson in laughter among the have-nots. And on that day we also learned about things like patience, wonder, and quirks of nature.

Like most Volunteers, I learned to nourish myself on just the basics, whether it was native foods or native wisdom. But that's a whole other story of survival, in some ways not so different from the journey of those five men who were adrift for months in the Pacific in a leaky boat.

Ron Arias (Peru 1963-64) is a senior correspondent for *People* Magazine, a former college professor and the author of two books, *Tamazunchale,* a novel which was nominated for the National Book Award, and *Five Against The Sea,* the nonfiction account of five Costa Rican fishermen's survival at sea. He lives in Stamford, Connecticut.

Uganda, East Africa

Raid on Entebbe, or My Three Days as a Mercenary

by Tina Thuermer

Our group was lucky: We won first prize—one week in Philadelphia. In the summer of 1973, 110 trainees bound for Zaire got to start their Peace Corps experience by spending a week in Philly preparing to be shipped out. We became overly familiar with Chestnut Street, Walnut Street, and all the other nuts in Philly—perhaps that's what hardened us for what was to come. I don't remember much from that week except a psychologist telling me not to expect my relationship with my boyfriend to last. He was wrong (we later got married). He was right (we later got divorced).

Our chartered plane took us first to England, and after a brief hiatus we took off for Uganda, where we stopped at Entebbe airport for refueling. While waiting there, we were privileged to watch Idi Amin giving a state send-off to President Bongo of Gabon. He also saw us, 110 still not too

scruffy but somewhat rumpled twenty-two-year-olds, with
a few forty- to sixty-year-olds thrown in for good measure.
Most of us, burned out on peace marches, were setting off
in an aura of cynicism to check out if there really was any
hope for the world and any way to avoid getting a nine-to-
five job. The ones with the stars in their eyes had gotten off
in Philadelphia after meeting the rest of us.

On the plane again, and ten minutes from Zaire's air-
space, the pilot told us he'd been ordered to turn back.
Unbeknownst to us, he'd been given the added incentive of
being blown out of the sky if he didn't comply. We arrived
back at Entebbe and spent four or five hours on the plane
having our passports examined by the military police. They
finally let us off the plane and corralled us into the lounge,
under heavy guard by machinegun-toting soldiers, where
they proceeded to search our baggage. One older fellow had
a bit of a hard time explaining why he had maps of a variety of African countries in his bags—they thought he was a
CIA spy. There was a great deal of puzzlement when a tam-
pon was unearthed, taken apart and discussed. They
dropped it like a hot potato when they found out what it was
for.

We ended up spending two nights on hard benches in
that airport. None of us had been bright enough to contact
the American embassy, but they finally figured out we were
there. Most of us were blithely unaware of the seriousness
of the situation. It was not until the reporters began to show
up that we realized we were international news. Cables
were flying between the Peace Corps, State Department,
and other governmental bodies. At home, there were stories
in the newspapers and anguished moms were interviewed
on TV weeping, "I told my son not to join that Peace
Corps." Meanwhile, back in Entebbe, we were entertaining
ourselves by playing Frisbee, sampling the delights of
African beer, and singing "Kumbaya" in the darker mo-
ments.

It seems Amin had decided we were Israeli mercenaries

(I mean, really, have you *seen* a Peace Corps Volunteer lately?) and was in intense communication with Nixon, Mobutu, and a variety of other heads of state to find out who we really were. It was exactly a year later that he pulled the same stunt with a group of Israelis, thus provoking the famous Raid on Entebbe.

The third day, we were allowed to go to the Lake Victoria Hotel. The last time I had been there was as an eleven-year-old on safari with my family. In memory of that trip, I sent the folks a postcard saying, "Having a wonderful time. Wish you were here." After we checked in, my roommate and I decided to lie down and take a brief nap. We woke up eighteen hours later—one of the best sleeps of my life.

The Marines arrived while we were sitting around the pool the next day waiting for news. I'd always had a jaundiced view of Marines, but these guys came bearing M & M's, cigarettes, and malaria pills and won our hearts. Their comments on the Ugandan populace also proved that during their time in Uganda they had acquired no cross-cultural skills.

Finally, we were released. When we arrived in Bukavu, at the Athenée that was to be a brand new training center for Peace Corps, we asked Willet Weeks and Frank Zappala, our directors, if they had been worried about us. Hell no, we were told, the mattresses had been delayed and our capture had given them time to get them there.

Welcome to Peace Corps.

Tina Thuermer (Zaire 1973-75) is principal of the Washington (D.C.) International Lower School. She has an Ed.D. in Education Administration from Columbia University Teachers College and is a professor in the education department of George Mason University.

Zaire, West Africa

I Had A Hero

by Mike Tidwell

Equipped with a motorcycle from the United States Agency for International Development and administrative support from the Zairian Department of Agriculture and Rural Development, I set out to show the people of Kalambayi something about fish culture. I was an extension agent for the government's *Projet Pisciculture Familiale.*

Six days a week, I left my house around 7 a.m. and rode as much as forty miles over unspeakably eroded dirt roads and down narrow paths. I visited villages and expounded the virtues of fish culture to anyone who would listen. "No thanks. We've got enough work to do already." Around six in the evening, exhausted from equal parts of sun and foreign language, I'd return home.

It was after a few weeks of this that I met Ilunga Mbumba, chief of the village of Ntita Kalambayi. I was riding my Yamaha 125 Enduro through an uninhabited stretch of bush when he appeared from out of the ten-foot-tall grass along the trail, signaling for me to stop. Had he not waved,

I'm pretty sure I would have stopped anyway. Ilunga had been out hunting antelope and he presented a sight worth inspecting. In one hand he carried a spear, in the other a crude machete. On his head was a kind of coonskin cap with a bushy tail hanging down in back. Around his neck was a string supporting a leather charm to ward off bad bush spirits. Two underfed mongrel dogs circled his bare feet, panting.

When I stopped and saw Ilunga that first time, I saw a man living, it seemed to me, in another century. Inside the tall grass from which he had just stepped, the clock ran a thousand years slow, if it registered any time at all. Unable to help myself, I stared at him openly, taking him in from head to toe. He, meanwhile, stared back at me with the same wide-eyed incredulity. And no wonder. With my ghost-white skin and rumbling motorcycle, with my bulging safety goggles and orange riding gloves, with my bushy brown beard flowing out from under a banana-yellow crash helmet—with all this, I suppose I had a lot of nerve thinking of *him* as a museum piece.

For a moment we just kept gawking, Ilunga and I, mentally circling each other, both of us trying to decide whether to burst out laughing or to run for safety. In the end, we did neither. We became friends.

"My name is Ilunga," he said, extending his hand.

"My name is Michel," I said, shaking it.

We smiled at each other another moment before Ilunga got around to telling me he had heard my job was to teach people how to raise fish. It sounded like something worth trying, he said, and he wondered if I would come by his village to help him look for a pond site. I said I would and took down directions to his house.

The next day the two of us set off into the bush, hunting for a place to raise fish.

"The first thing we need," I told Ilunga, "is water. Do you know a good spot where there's a small stream or a spring?"

"Follow me," he said.

Machetes in hand, we stomped and stumbled and hacked our way through the savanna grass for two hours before finding an acceptable site along a stream about a twenty-minute walk from Ilunga's village. Together, we paced off a pond and staked a water canal running between it and a point farther up the stream. Then, with a shovel I sold him on credit against his next corn harvest, Ilunga began a two-month journey through dark caverns of physical pain and overexertion. He began digging. No bulldozers here. The task of carving out a pond from the valley-bottom floor was left to the farmer himself.

There is no easy way to dig a fish pond with a shovel. You just have to do it. You have to place the tip to the ground, push the shovel in with your foot, pull up a load of dirt, and then throw the load twenty or thirty feet to the pond's edge. Then you have to do it again—tip to the ground, push it in, pull it up, throw the dirt. After you do this about 50,000 times, you have an average-size, ten- by fifteen-meter pond.

In many ways, the work is like a marathon. If you go too fast, you invite physical ruin. If you go too slow, you may never finish. You have to pace yourself. You have to dig a few hours each day, carefully spreading out the pain over time. But no matter what, you can't take a break. You can't stop. Not even for a week. To do so is to risk losing the rhythm of the fight and so become suddenly overwhelmed by the task at hand. Once the shovel enters the soil the first time, the work must continue every day—tip to the ground, push it in, pull it up, throw the dirt—again and again, meter by meter, 50,000 times, until the marathon is over.

But Ilunga, being a chief and all, wasn't content with an average-size pond. He wanted one almost twice that size. He wanted a pond fifteen by twenty meters. I told him he was crazy as we measured it out. I repeated the point with added conviction after watching him use his bare foot to drive the thin shovel blade into the ground.

"A pond this big is too much work for one person," I said. "It'll kill you."

"See you next week," he said.

"It's too much, Ilunga."

He started digging.

"Okay," I said. "*Bonne chance.*"

I left him at the pond site and began heading toward the village, hearing every ten seconds as I walked away the sound of a shovel-load of dirt hitting the ground after traveling twenty feet through the air.

For me, it was painful visiting Ilunga each week. This was the part of the fish culture process I had been dreading ever since arriving. I'd come to check on the pond's progress and find Ilunga grunting and shoveling and pitching dirt the same way I had left him the week before. I winced each time his foot pushed the shovel into the ground. I groaned inwardly at the sight of his clothes, ragged, full of yawning holes that revealed a glistening, overworked body. I calculated that to finish the pond he would have to move a total of 4,000 cubic feet of dirt. Guilt gnawed at me. This was no joke. He really was going to kill himself.

One week I couldn't stand it any longer. I found Ilunga at the pond site with his body covered with the usual mixture of dirt and sweat.

"Give me the shovel," I told him.

"Oh no, Michel," he said. "This work is too much for you."

"Give it to me," I repeated, a bit indignantly. "Take a rest."

He shrugged and handed me the shovel. I began digging. Okay, I thought, tip to the ground, push it in, pull it up, throw the dirt. I did it again. It wasn't nearly as hard as I had thought. Stroke after stroke, I kept going. About twenty minutes later, though, it got hot. I began wondering how, at 8:30 in the morning, the sun had suddenly reached noontime intensity. I paused to take off my shirt. Ilunga, thinking I was quitting, jumped up and reached for the shovel.

"No, no," I said. "I'm still digging. Sit down."

He shrugged again and said that since I was apparently serious about digging, he was going to go check on one of his fields. "Good idea," I said.

Shirtless, alone, I carried on. Tip to the ground, push it in, pull it up, throw the dirt. An hour passed. Tip to the ground, push it in, pull it up...throw...throw the...dammit, throw the dirt. My arms were signaling that they didn't like tossing dirt over such a great distance. It hurts, they said. Stop making us do it. But I couldn't stop. I had been digging a paltry hour and a half. I was determined to go on, to help Ilunga. How could I expect villagers to do work I was incapable of doing myself?

Sweat gathered on my forehead and streamed down my face as I continued, shoveling and shoveling. About thirty minutes passed and things started to get really ugly. My body buckled with fatigue. My back and shoulders joined my arms in screaming for an end to hostilities. I was no longer able to throw the dirt. Instead, I carried each load twenty feet and ignobly spooned it onto the dike. I was glad Ilunga wasn't around to see this. It was embarrassing. And God was it hot. The hottest day I could ever remember. Even occasional breezes rustling through the surrounding savanna grass didn't help. And then I looked at my hands. Both palms had become blistered. One was bleeding.

I took a short break and began digging again. The pain resumed, cracking out all over my body. Fifteen minutes later, my hands finally refused to grip the shovel. It fell to the ground. My back then refused to bend down to allow my arms the chance to refuse to pick it up. I was whipped. After just two hours of digging, I was incapable of doing any more. With a stiff, unnatural walk, I went over to the dike. Ilunga had just returned, and I collapsed next to him.

"I think I'll stop now," I managed, unable to hide my piteous state. "Take over if you want."

He did. He stood up, grabbed the shovel and began working—smoothly, confidently, a man inured to hard work. Tip to the ground, push it in, pull it up, throw the dirt. Lying on my side, exhausted, I watched Ilunga. Then I looked hard at the spot where I had been digging. I had done nothing. The pond was essentially unchanged. I had moved perhaps thirty cubic feet of dirt. That meant 3,970 cubic feet for Ilunga.

After the brief digging experience, my weekly visits to the pond became even more painful and my awe of Ilunga grew. Day after day, four or five hours each day, he kept going. He kept digging his pond. He worked like a bull and never complained. Not once. Not when he hit a patch of gravel-size rocks that required a pickaxe and extra sweat. Not when, at the enormous pond's center, he had to throw each shovel-load twice to reach the dikes. And not when he became ill.

His hand was on fire one morning when I arrived and shook it.

"You're sick," I said.

"I know," he said and resumed digging.

"Then quit working and get some rest."

"I can't," came the reply. "I've got to finish this pond."

Several weeks later, Ilunga drove his shovel into the earth and threw its load one last time. I never thought it would happen, but there it was: Ilunga's pond, huge, fifteen by twenty meters, and completely finished. We hollowed out a bamboo inlet pipe and positioned it in the upper dike so canal water could enter the pond. Three days later, the pond was gloriously full of water. Using my motorcycle and two ten-liter carrying *bidons,* I transported stocking fish from another project post twenty miles to the south. When the last of the 300 tilapia fingerlings had entered the new pond, I turned to Ilunga and shook his hand over and over again. We ran around the banks hooting and hollering, laughing like children, watching the fish and marveling at what a wonderful thing a pond was. Where before there had been nothing, just grass and scrub trees, had come watery life.

To celebrate, I had brought a bottle of *tshitshampa,* the local home brew, and Ilunga and I began pouring each other shots and slapping each other on the back and talking entirely too loud for two men sitting alone on a pond bank in the middle of the African bush. A warm glow spread from our stomachs to our limbs and, soon, strongly, our heads. Ilunga expressed his dream of digging three, no six, no twelve more fish ponds, and I concluded that there was no biological reason why, if fed properly, tilapia couldn't grow to be the size of Land Rovers. At one point, we decided to assign names to all of Ilunga's fish. Straight-faced, signaling each other to be quiet, we crouched next to the water and began naming the first few fish that swam by. After four fish, though, we lost track of which fish had which names. This struck us as absolutely hilarious for some reason, and we fell on our backs and stamped our feet and laughed so hard we couldn't stand it.

Oh, sweet joy, the pond was finished. Ilunga had done it. He had taken my instructions and accomplished a considerable thing. And on that day when we finally stocked the pond, I knew that no man would ever command more respect from me than one who, to better feed his children, moves 4,000 cubic feet of dirt with a shovel.

I had a hero.

Mike Tidwell (Zaire 1985-87) is the author of *The Ponds of Kalambayi,* a book about his Peace Corps experience which won the 1991 Paul Cowan Prize given by *RPCV Writers & Readers.* He is also author of *In The Shadow of the White House: Drugs, Death, and Redemption on the Streets of the Nation's Capital,* and the recipient of a 1994 National Endowment for the Arts Creative Writing fellowship. He graduated magna cum laude with a B.A. in political science from the University of Georgia and now lives in Takoma Park, Maryland.

Hungary, Eastern Europe

From Leningrad to Budapest

by Jeffrey Taylor

I fear I've become a bit of a crotchety, contemptuous, old expatriate here as Eastern Europe gets progressively diluted by more starchy Americans come to see "all the changes." I already catch myself beginning too many sentences with "I remember when...." When every sign still read People's Republic, and my school sat on Red Army Street. When only Germans drove Western cars, and Hungarians still bought Trabants new. When an establishment distinguished itself by advertising its private ownership. Most of all, I can remember when Soviet soldiers in Hungary actually wore all the pins and hats and helmets that tourists buy on Buda's Castle Hill. I remember when the Soviet Union was still a monolith on our Eastern border, and I traveled through it only months before it slipped away into history.

A month after I arrived at my site, the English department at my school was invited to visit our sister school in Tallin, Estonia. The Estonians were planning to hold Finno-

Ugric Days with us and their sister Finnish school. (A fact only linguists seem to know is that Hungarian is related to only two other modern languages, Finnish and Estonian. While those two languages are quite similar to each other—Estonian children are reared on Finnish TV—contemporary Hungarian has little in common with them since the tribes split up a few thousand years ago.) The Estonians had planned a big get-together, and we would use the opportunity to practice English, Eastern Europe's new *lingua franca*.

We organized fourteen of our exemplary English students, and the three English teachers, Eva, Janos, and me, plus one of our Russian teachers, Magdi. Magdi and Eva, who'd also taught Russian, would prove that they knew best how to approach each slide the trip took toward catastrophe. They laughed deliriously.

Once on our way, I settled into my short bunk and prepared to wait out the two-and-a-half-day, not-altogether uncomfortable trip to Leningrad. The train had curtains that were decorated with "1917," "October Revolution," and pictures of battleships. I shamelessly stole a set.

At the border, the guards rapidly stamped the Hungarian passports, and then stared at mine. They looked at me, then the passport picture, then the visa, then did the circle again. Even at this late date in the Cold War, they couldn't accept that Americans were crossing this remote border post so conveniently, but after looking long enough, they acknowledged that everything was indeed in order. The train then sat for another ten hours waiting for a crane to lift our car and set it on new axles—Soviet rails are wider than those in the rest of Europe.

The Estonians seemed genuinely thrilled that an American had come along—none of them had ever met a native speaker. Yet their British lilts were perfect, and they knew precisely how to use many idioms, like "make yourself at home" and "no room to swing a cat." (I'd never heard that one before.)

The return trip provided more interest because we rode with a group of students from the Leningrad Rail School. One young man, who aspired to be a disco DJ, optimistically anticipated selling in Hungary an electric iron, a car clock, and twenty packs of Russian cigarettes in order to buy a Japanese radio.

At one stop, the group took me to visit the Ukrainian town of L'vov, a decaying Hapsburg city with yellow trams, gaudy baroque churches, and an opera house square. A cafe closed as we approached because the Rail School students were speaking Russian. They didn't dare speak at all in the opera square because a gathering of Ukrainians was loudly proclaiming the abuses of Russian rule. Back in the train station, a ten-foot-tall statue of Lenin had been hidden by an equally tall palm tree. As had the Estonians, the Ukrainians sensed that independence would be only a few nudges farther.

As we traveled through Russia, I noticed many things about the countryside. Every body of water—even roadside puddles—was brown and usually bubbled at its edges with some sick foam. Towns seemed literally broken. Cement walkways rotted and led off to abrupt ends. People walked on dirt paths that crossed yards, fields, and rails at obtuse angles to get to those rare enterprises that were still performing some useful service. And although this claim seems excessive, I honestly did not see the sun once while in the Soviet Union. Not for ten days. Immediately, though, on crossing into democratic Hungary, the sun rebelled, burst through the stodgy clouds, and illuminated the small gardens hanging lush with fall fruits. I had to concede that the John Birchers were actually right—the sun never shines in communist countries.

Returning to Hungary, though, had seemed like an unlikely prospect for much of our visit. Before departing Hungary, we'd bought our round trip tickets for the ridiculous price of approximately $12. We hadn't known that tickets were idle scraps of paper without reservations. We had secured reservations into Russia, but the return reservations could be made only in Leningrad.

Before creating hell, God created the Leningrad train station as practice. When we arrived there, we spent six hours waiting for the Estonians to pick us up. The station had features that were as pointless as those in the disintegrating towns along the rails—big doors led nowhere, but the minor one, in a corner under some wooden stairs, opened into the cavernous waiting room; of some thirty ticket windows, two were operating, and they weren't selling reservations to Budapest. The hall was nevertheless filled. Travelers squeezed onto the benches or stood. Yet I can't remember anyone speaking or reading. They looked blankly at their bags or straight ahead. One corner had a buffet selling slices of bread and sardines, and a few queued for them. Surrounding the train station was a market of semilegitimate black-market stalls. They sold eggs at two rubles and packets of Camels (from R. J. Reynolds famous tobacco airlift) for sixteen rubles, all at a time when a monthly salary was 250 rubles.

When Ingvar, the Estonian school's headmaster, arrived to pick us up, even he thought our lack of return reservations was a hopeless situation. He informed us that all the trains to Budapest were completely reserved until January.

Our sister school's village, Loo, was actually a few kilometers from Tallin, and "village" might be a misnomer. Loo had a chicken cooperative where everyone worked, and which accounted for the village's relative prosperity. Even Soviet industry couldn't ruin a chicken—in any economy, it had absolute value. The town had about fifty uniform apartment blocks and a store that sold very little. Envious city dwellers, however, would travel to Loo to try to bribe someone to allow them to shop for the canned fish and dubious sausages available there.

Every evening we laughed ourselves to sleep, thinking we weren't getting back to Hungary until January. We stayed one day past our planned return date, and it looked like we were there for many more, when we received a message from Ingvar in Leningrad that we could leave—he had gotten us reservations.

As the train began rolling, Eva and Magdi were shedding tears from the force of their laughter, and each kept prodding the other on to more by howling about chickens and eggs. My Hungarian wasn't so good at this point, and I thought they might be speaking in some sort of folk dialect, but then Eva translated for me. Ingvar had gone to the director of the Railroads, demanded reservations, and set two chickens and twenty-four eggs on his desk.

I remember when a couple of chickens and two dozen eggs could get eighteen people from Leningrad to Budapest.

Jeffrey Taylor (Hungary 1990-92) was an English teacher in Mohacs, Hungary, where he worked at a Hungarian gymnasium and a school for Croatian refugees. Taylor has an M.A. in history from the Central European University in Budapest and a B.A. from Oberlin College in English and Politics.

Tonga, South Pacific

Under the Tongan Sun

by Tina Martin

Ilived in a tiny hut made of bamboo and coconut leaves and lined with dozens of mats, pieces of tapa cloth, and wall-to-wall children. When I sat on the floor with my back against the back door, my feet almost touched the front door. There was no electricity or running water, so I used a kerosene lamp and drew water from the well. There were breadfruit trees and avocado trees around my hut, and if I wanted a coconut, the children climbed a tree for me.

The kids I taught were always with me, and I loved them even more than I once loved my privacy. I always wanted to have children, but I never thought I'd have so many and so soon. These were the children I would like to see back home—children who had never even seen a television set and didn't depend upon "things" for their entertainment because they didn't have any things. For fun, they taught each other dances and songs, and they juggled oranges.

They woke me up in the morning, calling through my bamboo poles. They took my five sentini and got me freshly baked bread from the shop across the lawn, and they helped me eat it. Some of them watched the ritual of my morning bath—water drawn from the well and heated on my kerosene stove and poured into a tin, then over a pre-soaped me. They sometimes braided my hair and helped me get dressed for school. Then they walked me there, where I used the oral English method we learned in training—acting out the language so there's no need for translation.

"I'm running! I'm running!" I said as I ran in front of the class. "I'm running. I'm running!" I took a child by the hand.

"Run!" I said, and eventually he did. The goal was to have a running paradigm, which usually ended. "I running, you running, he/she/it running." We did this for all verbs. English was the link between Tonga and other land masses. And English was the exercise that kept me scrawny, the worst physical defect a body could have in the Tongan culture, where fat was beautiful. I tried to compensate for my lack of bulk by being very *anga lelei* (good-natured), which was their most cherished personality trait.

After school the children would come home with me and stay, singing Tongan songs and the ones I'd taught them.

Then I tried to help them prepare for the sixth grade exam that would determine their scholastic future. And they helped me prepare whichever vegetable was to be my dinner.

The children never left until I was safely tucked into bed under my canopy of mosquito net on top of tapa cloth. Then I blew out my lamp, lay down, and listened to songs from a kava ceremony nearby. Sometimes there was light from what a Tongan teacher told me was now the American moon, since we had put a man there. On moonless nights, I fell asleep in complete darkness. But I fell asleep knowing that I would always wake up under the Tongan sun.

Tina Martin (Tonga 1969-71) began her career in English as a Second Language as a teacher trainer in Tonga, then went on to teach in Spain and in Algeria. She is now an ESL instructor at City College of San Francisco.

Nepal, South Asia

"H" Is For Hopsi

by Jacqueline Francis

First things first: I am not angry...most of the time. What use is it to be mad at a country of 17 million? Just because many Nepali folks upon first sight of me, or anyone else who is obviously of African descent, feel compelled to say, "*Hopsi,*" which is, after all, the Nepali word for Negro. One English-Nepali dictionary says this, in its entry for *Hopsi,* "Member of black skinned, wooly haired, flat-nosed and thick-lipped African race." Apparently "*Hopsi*" didn't start off as a slur, a chant of ridicule, a soundless utterance from the lips of every passerby; it's just that way now, a case in point of one word's evolution.

When some Nepalis see me, they experience a moment of self-congratulation for being able to distinguish a black foreigner from the larger group of white and Mongoloid ones. There is sincere wonderment in their eyes because seeing me is like sighting a snow leopard or some other rare, only-read-about-in-books creature.

It's true—not many black people of any nationality pass through Nepal. In two years, I've seen five other blacks, all but one a tourist, in addition to those of us who work in Nepal and are part of the expatriate community. That includes an average of two to three of us Peace Corps Volunteers, two to three marines assigned to the U.S. Embassy, and embassy and U.S. mission officials and their families.

You can imagine the excitement of some Nepalis who see a black person walking towards them on the road. They can hardly believe their good luck, I suppose. Once I saw a Nepali woman point at me and another black Peace Corps Volunteer, as if to say to the toddler cradled in her arms, "Son, they are members of a black-skinned, wooly haired, flat-nosed and thick-lipped African race. Try to remember what they look like." In all fairness, however, when I have asked Nepali Peace Corps staff why the stares, they say it isn't meant to be hurtful. It's just, "Look at that person."

Another black Peace Corps Volunteer told me he once found himself in the middle of a haircut at a barbershop—a harrowing experience in itself—when the power went off. In the darkened shop, curious Nepalis who had been content just staring got bold: They ran their fingers over his hair, and he heard more than one of them say, "It's like a sponge!"

This kind of attention is not born of admiration, but instead, of a lack of familiarity and gory fascination. We're talking the proverbial car wreck that you can't take your eyes off.

And Nepalis have no monopoly on this—every once in a while, one of my braver nonblack American friends will say, "How do you do your hair?" "Do you wash it?" etc. After all, you just don't see much of that on American TV.

As a result, white Americans sometimes forget that America is not all white. I've heard white Peace Corps Volunteers use "white" as a synonym for "foreigners," e.g.,

"Nepalis stare at Americans because they have never seen white people" or, "Sometimes I just want to see a white face." Well, where do I fit in here or don't I?

I packed a naive expectation next to my Walkman and my wool socks when I readied myself for Nepal: It was that there would be a bond between myself and all Nepalis, we people of color. Ironically, I am a brown-skinned person living in a country of mostly brown-skinned people and I've heard only twice in two years, "You're just like us." Not only that, but black foreigners are often targets of pointed disrespect: kids running after me screaming, *"Hopsi! Hopsi!,"* punks laughing at me, singing, "I am a disco dancer" and trying to break-dance; older Nepalis who refuse to believe that I am American because I am black.

Initially, I was concerned that verbal taunts would give way to physical violence, that a bad Nepali person was going to hurt me because I was black. For a long time, I always carried my passport everywhere with me: I figured that the USA stamp would be my shield. But no one has ever laid a threatening hand on me in Nepal. My fears were unwarranted.

Nepalis living in the rural hill areas, as do Peace Corps staff, have always treated me as an honored guest of their country. No one has ever tossed the "H" word in my face in those communities. Most unpleasant incidents I've faced in urban areas—Nepal's big cities and district centers. The Terai—the plains of Nepal—is a notoriously tough place for black people to live. There, dark-skinned Nepalis and Indians put up with daily harassment. I consider myself fortunate to work and live in the foothills of mid-western Nepal.

I wish I had shared my hurt and fears with my PCV friends from the beginning. My first months in Nepal, I lived my life like a loaded gun—there were a lot of negative feelings and pain bottled up inside of me. To be honest, I was disappointed that my white PCV friends ignored the comments tossed at me when we walked through the bazaars—I wanted them to confront those Nepalis who harassed me, and they didn't. But then, neither did I.

I suspect that *"Hopsi"* is not a hateful slur to Nepalis, not the same as nigger. Instead, it's just another hierarchical classification of the caste system, like Brahmin, Magar, Rai, Kammi, etc. These days, some Nepalis who watched the 1988 Olympic Games in Seoul on television congratulate me on the performance of all the black athletes who racked up medals. Another Nepali woman said she really admired the way my *jaat* could sing (Michael Jackson is a tee-shirt hero here). They're all trying to be nice, but it makes me uncomfortable. In Nepal, I've changed my self perception: I am a black person first, a woman second. It used to be the other way around.

Frankly, I've come to no firm resolutions about this part of my experience. *"Hopsi"* still hurts, although sometimes it rolls off my back. I've stayed, I think, because good times, good people outnumber the bad.

Jacqueline Francis (Nepal 1987-89) was a TEFL teacher and teacher trainer posted in Surkhet District. In 1993 she completed an M.A. in African-American Studies at the University of Wisconsin-Madison. Currently, she is living in Atlanta, Georgia with her partner, and studying for a Ph.D. in art history at Emory University.

Niger, West Africa

Learning the African Protocols

by Denise Voelker

Leaving the San Francisco Paramedic Corps for the Peace Corps was not an easy decision. But after ten years of giving my heart and soul to the streets, burnout was becoming my constant companion. I was determined to cut that umbilical cord that binds every paramedic to the wild adventure and startling sadness of street medicine. I found, however, that paramedics don't retire easily.

As I packed for Africa, emergency medicine books kept creeping into my luggage. I wondered if there was a twelve-step program for adrenaline junkies, or if I'd ever stop noticing good veins when I shook hands with people. But I knew it was time for a change, so, despite the siren song of the streets, I was off to Africa—Niger, West Africa, to be precise, smack in the center of the proverbial end of the earth, just a bus ride away from Timbuktu and about two hunded years away from the twentieth century.

The Peace Corps assigned me to be a forester, though my background is remarkably devoid of forestry skills of any kind. I decided not to argue with the Feds and dedicated myself to learning the anatomy and physiology of African trees. Our training was rigorous—11 hours a day, six days a week, for three months—in a rambling, cinder-block facility located in the village of Hamdallaye.

Besides intense tree school, we immersed ourselves in French and tribal dialect language classes, gardening, agriculture and local customs. I even learned to ride a motorcycle, becoming one of the Peace Corps' newest Sahel's Angels.

During the first week of training, while dodging goats, camels, and heatstroke, I began to get sentimental about my nice, safe ambulance job. I missed the crazies—both in and out of uniform. In the nighttime silence of Hamdallaye, I'd sort through the hundreds of ambulance calls I'd run, remembering the thousands of lives I had the privilege to touch.

I missed medicine, so I guess it was only a matter of time until I slid back into the blood-and-guts mode to play paramedic again. Certainly seeing my first camel bite got the Code 3 juices flowing. I worried about where one would go with a serious injury and how ill-equipped most Volunteers would be to deal with such an emergency on their own.

Our training period would end soon, and the Peace Corps would be placing us far and wide across Niger, into remote bush villages and farming communities. I was amazed at the distances Volunteers would need to travel to get even primary care in the event of an emergency. A casual poll of my fellow trainees produced only a handful of souls with even a CPR card. With the camel bite memory fresh in my mind, I approached the Peace Corps about creating emergency first aid training for my fellow Volunteers.

Because of the incredible work load, Peace Corps training is as structured as boot camp. Though our training director was enthusiastic about my idea, she could find minimal free time in our already crowded schedule. I came away with a whopping two-hour time slot, and three days to prepare my class—two hours to train novices to deal with an emergency where the closest medical attention might be twenty-four hours away by ox cart! Coming from the land of the four-minute response goal and rapid delivery to a trauma center, it was a moment of reality check for me— this was everyday life in a Third World country and, as a Peace Corps Volunteer, I had accepted these risks. I wanted to draw on my experience as a professional disaster chaser, to design a class that might really help the Volunteer faced with a medical emergency.

Facing the hard, cold facts that an injury might require long and uncomfortable transport, I concentrated on packaging. There was also a heavy emphasis on environmental injuries and recognizing when there's trouble with a closed wound. I took it for granted that the local chiefs wouldn't be sticklers about legal issues, so I left the intricacies of the Good Samaritan Act alone. The temptation was to include everything, but my two-hour time limit kept me to the basics.

The class went off without a hitch, covering transport comfort in a donkey cart and using locally woven baskets as splints. With average summer temperatures of 110^0F to 120^0F, we spent a lot of time discussing heat. Given the distances and primitive reality of the place, we spent no time on CPR.

Months later, word drifted back to me via the Peace Corps bush telegraph system that a Volunteer in the remote desert post of Agadez treated an open fracture using information he managed to retain from our short class. Other success stories drifted my way from time to time. These Volunteers dealt with some fairly serious trauma under extremely primitive conditions; I would have been proud to share an ambulance with any of them.

Denise Voelker (Niger 1989-92) was a coordinator of an agricultural development program in Western Niger, supervising Volunteer projects as diverse as maternal/child health, well-digging and sheep husbandry. She is a writer, with a M.A. in Community Development and a B.A. in Geography.

The Gambia, West Africa

Reasons for Joy

by Victoria Derr

My first memory of Amenata is one of my first memories of life in Kani Kunda. It was a sunny, soaking-wet day at the end of the rainy season. Still unconfident about communicating in Mandinka, I was blundering through a conversation with our landlady, Bakoto, when Amenata came for a visit. After exchanging a few greetings with her, it became abundantly clear that Amenata was ten going on thirty-five and wanted that fact known to her new neighbor.

"Why didn't you come to our compound at night?" Amenata asked and, without pausing for a response, went on to tell me that Mr. Njie, the infallible former Volunteer in Kani Kuna, had gone to their compound every night to tutor the school children.

"Mr. Njie could speak perfect Mandinka," she added. "You can't speak Mandinka at all.

"Mr. Njie spent every waking hour in the village. Mr. Njie never stayed in his house. Mr. Njie went to discos with us. Mr. Njie gave us pencils."

Mr. Njie. Mr. Njie. Mr. Njie.

This kind of criticism would become very familiar to me in my two years. Many Gambians wanted to decide what every Peace Corps Volunteer *should* do, not willing to recognize that, just like themselves, we were individuals. But Amenata's content with Mr. Njie and contempt for me was the first of such blatant criticisms, and it stung.

As time went on, though, Amenata and I became good friends. I was an ally in a male-dominated world and, more than that, a release from her work. Amenata Darboe was the oldest girl in a family of seven children. As her two mothers were often busy with the garden and rice fields, Amenata was left with raising her five younger siblings. She carried water, sometimes six or seven large buckets in the morning and again at night, pounded rice, swept, washed clothes, cleaned, and cooked.

Amenata had a wonderful work ethic. She took her work seriously, took pride in doing it well. But every now and then she would dash over to my house, seeking refuge from pounding or cooking dinner. Her mothers, Anna and Neema, would call her. With mischievous eyes and smile, Amenata would shrug, telling me to let it go. And, being an old softy, I did.

One of Amenata's tricks, and she was full of them, was to sneak up to the house and scare the living daylights out of me. In the late afternoons, I often read outside in the back yard, which was separated from Amenata's compound only by a shoulder-high woven-reed fence. It was peaceful out back. With its eastern exposure, I was shaded from the hot afternoon sun and could sit in my sling-back chair, waiting for the evening breezes to cool me off. And somehow, despite the sounds of cows, donkeys, chickens, children, and pounding—that steady thump of wood hitting wood—I escaped into the world of my book.

"NEEMA BIYAAY!!!" Amenata would shriek my Gambian name, bringing me back with near heart failure into the world of Kani Kunda. It would take me a good long minute to recover; then I would start to look for Amenata.

It didn't take me long, though, for she had gotten just the reaction she was looking for and would be lying on the opposite side of the fence, rolling in laughter and delight. At times like this, I would remember the true goals of Volunteers: Goal number one was to entertain Gambians, goal number two was to teach, and the second was a lot harder than the first.

"*M foo alimetoo,*" she would slyly demand.

"What?" I would ask. There were some words I could never remember, no matter how often I heard them, and alimetoo (match) was one of those.

"Matchoo. Matchoo." Amenata would say with contempt. "I'm going to cook." She didn't hide her dismay at the fact that I wasn't a Mandinka genius, but she tolerated it. After all, she did want a match.

Shaking my head and laughing, I'd go into the kitchen to get a few matches. Why did I give her matches when she scared me nearly to death? Why did I give her matches when they were only twenty-five *bututs* (quite affordable for a family with electricity and a motorbike—more than I had)? And why did I give her matches when she demanded them so adamantly? The only reason I could ever conceive was that her delight was infectious: She made me laugh, even if at my own expense. And after a long day of two hundred Form 1 students, that laughter was worth a whole lot more than twenty-five bututs.

During my two years in the Gambia I watched Amenata grow and change; Amenata was transforming into a woman before my eyes. She experienced incredible growth spurts, becoming embarrassed as she outgrew more and more of her clothes.

One starlit night on my back porch, as I shared my dinner with friends Botto and Bakary, we heard Amenata's family talking about me. Anna and Amenata were explaining to Neema why, at age twenty-three, I was not married. Things are different in America, they said. Our conversation out back shifted to the same. I said I felt sorry for Amenata's husband, whoever he would be, because Amenata would be the most stubborn wife imaginable.

Botto commented that soon, very soon, Amenata would be married: Her time had come. *Married!?* I couldn't believe it! Not Amenata! Not now!

"But Amenata is still afraid of men," I replied, picturing her shy face. Just that evening she had hid behind my skirt at the well as I greeted some student-aged village men.

"Yes, Tori," Botto explained, "but that's exactly what her family is hoping for, to marry her while she is still young and afraid of men, so that she may bring her family honor."

It broke my heart to think of it. Amenata was wild. Her spirit and her laughter, her *childhood*, gave her tremendous freedom, tremendous joy. She liked to *play* house and took on its responsibilities most of the time, but it was not her compound. If she did not cook the food, no husband would blame her. She could still sneak to my front yard for a ten-minute respite from her chores. Marriage would change all that. *I* wasn't ready for that change. I couldn't imagine how Amenata must feel, knowing that each day as her body blossomed and changed, she was one day closer to marriage. I pictured tired women, striding home from the rice fields, bent over dinner in smoky cooking huts, resting on mats under the mango. Amenata would become this. The images didn't settle well with me. She was too vital to be burdened with *life*.

The next morning, as I was sipping my first cup of bitter Nescafe, Amenata gracefully appeared at my door, with a neighbor's baby tied to her back. She was beaming, and I realized that Amenata was always beaming when she had a child in her arms.

"Do you want to have children, Amenata?" Dumb question, I thought, since this was not really a conscious decision in Gambian women's lives, but her response was just what I was looking for. As she assuredly nodded her head yes, she pulled the baby to her lap, his hand grasping her finger, and the longing, the love, in her face told me that it would be all right. That though Amenata was ten years my junior, she was far more ready to assume the roles of motherhood than I. She would be ready to relinquish childhood.

I smiled that she would soon have her own child to hold, her own house to run. Perhaps soon Amenata would no longer roll on the ground in laughter at the crazy white lady next door, but I knew that she would have *different* reasons for joy, and that those reasons created the beauty, not the burden, of life.

Victoria Derr (The Gambia 1990-92) taught high school science, math and English in Mansakonko, The Gambia. Derr is currently working toward an M.A. at Yale University, School of Forestry and Environmental Studies, and is editor of *TRI News,* the journal of the Tropical Resources Institute. She received a B.A. in biology and writing from Hope College, in her home state of Michigan.

Morocco, North Africa

Three Lessons

by Craig Storti

Septentber. Sunset. The town of Safi, Morocco. I was washing dishes in my sink. From the minaret in the mosque three doors down came the evening prayer call, a song actually, blaring out of the loudspeakers, stopping the faithful in their tracks, turning them toward the East, sending them to their knees. To my ears, the cadence, the rhythm, the tone were all wrong, about as musical as a burglar alarm. I remember my words as I turned to my roommate: "Even *they* can't think that's pretty." I had been in Morocco four months.

Eight months later I was walking a friend to the bus station where she would catch the express to Casablanca. It was quiet, just before dawn, no horizon to speak of yet. No one else was about. From somewhere behind us, the muezzin's prayer call floated out over the silence, was answered from a nearby quarter, and then came at us faintly from several miles off to the south. The beauty of the chant stayed my step; I had to be still and listen. And then I remembered what I had said in September.

It was then I grasped my first Peace Corps lesson: You can accommodate the strange, the unusual, even the very unpleasant and make some kind of peace with it. You are not irrevocably the way you started out. With a little luck, you can grow.

Backpackers, hikers, and all manner of latter-day mountain men and women won't think much of the following story, but consider that it happened to a guy who, before his Peace Corps staging in Philadelphia, had always slept under a roof, in a bed, eschewed picnics, and never owned a sleeping bag. But who bought one at the same staging in Philadelphia (a cheap, cotton-lined number with green-hued scenes of deer in a forest, scenes that kept coming off on my underwear in the damp Safi spring).

In the spring of 1972, four of us rented a car and drove over the Tiz'n Tichka pass in the High Atlas Mountains down to the desert. We pulled up one night, just as the sun set behind the Jbel des Saghro in a place called Agdz. French tourists had filled the only hotel, but we could sleep on the floor of the cafe if we liked. I didn't like, but there was no choice.

The floor was cement, unrelentingly hard. I tried to lie in such a way that the greatest percentage of the softest parts of my body were between me and the cement, tried to become my own cushion. I thought I would never fall asleep, but I did.

And woke with the light. Not exactly refreshed and renewed, but exhilarated all the same. I had slept on a cement floor! That was my second lesson, courtesy of the Corps: how to do without. In that instance, a bed. In others, a bath or a shower, hot water, a refrigerator. Peace Corps whittles away your list of necessities. And when you consider that these are the things you can't live without, that you live in fear of not having, that you would fight to keep—then you understand that you can only be as free as that last list is short.

The scene is a cafe in Tangiers. Tomorrow is Saturday. I've just invited a Moroccan friend to a picnic at the beach. Will he come? "Perhaps," he says in English, translating from the Arabic, *N'shallah,* which literally means "God willing." And I'm feeling hurt. What does he mean perhaps? Either he wants to come or he doesn't. It's up to him. And if he doesn't want to come, he only has to say so. He doesn't understand why I'm upset. And I don't quite grasp "Perhaps." Our two cultures confront each other across the tea cups.

Only several years later did I understand. He would come, he meant, if Allah willed it. His wanting to come and his being able to come were not one and the same. In Morocco, unlike America, where there's a will there's not necessarily a way. So who was I to demand an answer to my question? And who was he to give one? When I understood this—and realized how strange he would find my ethic—I had learned my third lesson: I saw we can't confidently speak of truth, only truths, and I understood the power of culture. It was as if I had discovered a parallel universe, one founded upon a different auxiliary verb, on *may* rather than *will.* And where there was one different universe, might there not be others?

But the feeling wasn't at all what I expected; in embracing the possibility of countless other world views I should have loosened my grasp on my own. But instead I embraced it with renewed confidence, not in its rightness, of course, but appreciating anew the need to have a perspective—your own perspective—on the world in order to entertain the possibility of others.

Craig Storti (Morocco 1970-72) is the author of two books in the intercultural field—*The Art of Crossing Cultures* and *Cross-Cultural Dialogues*—one volume of popular history, *Incident At Bitter Creek,* and *A Few Minor Adjustments.* He lives in Washington, D.C and runs his own intercultural communications training business.

Ethiopia, Horn of Africa

So This Is Paris

by Kathleen Coskran

The year Detroit burned, I taught English and algebra in Dilla, Ethiopia. There were four of us *ferenjis* in Dilla that year. Doug, from Michigan, saved all the clippings from *The Christian Science Monitor* that his mother sent him about the riots and brought them out whenever a student asked him about his country.

He would unfold the dark pictures of burning buildings and say, "This is my home."

"He reads too much," Dick said. Dick didn't have time to read. He never missed a soccer, basketball, or volleyball game with the students or a chance to spend an hour at *Negussie Beit,* the only bar in Dilla with a refrigerator.

Our students called Claudie their mother because she stayed at school long after the sun went down to talk to them, help them with their homework, or give them advice. The day she bandaged Hamid's infected arm, he asked if she had ever been Scout.

"Yes, I was," she said.

"I thought so, miss, because you are always prepared."

The seventy-five students in 7-A, my homeroom, were proud of me because I knew their names in alphabetical

Addiswork Bekele to Zeudi Memedin. They called us all the Peace Corps, with the emphasis on the final p.

We walked down to the post office after school on a clay road that sucked at our shoes in the rainy season and streaked our clothes with dust in the dry season. We passed kids shouting *ferenj* (foreigner) at us, stepped around sheep and goats crossing the main drag, stopped to admire the professional mourners in a funeral procession, paused so the water man rolling his massive barrel up the hill from the river wouldn't lose momentum. As the barrel rumbled past and the mourners took up their ululations again, and a six-year-old ran up, tagged him, and dashed back to his friends, Dick would spread his arms wide and say, "So *this* is Paris."

That year school began with a chalk shortage. Students often asked for the chalk at the end of class, but I used every piece down to the last grain. There was none to spare. I also kept the fingernails on my right hand short to avoid spine-raising screeches on the blackboard and to get full use out of every piece. One day I had used a piece of blue chalk down to a shadow of color. Zelalem, from my sixth grade English class, asked me for the chalk after class, so I gave him this blue nothing and told him to save it for me. Like the man and his two talents, Zelalem gave me back twice as much chalk the next day. Somewhere he had found a grain of white chalk the same size as my spent blue piece. When I walked in the next morning, he opened his hand and presented me with two specks of chalk for the class. The pieces were so small that he would have lost them if he had set them down anywhere. He must have held the chalk in his hand all night.

A few weeks later, in that same class, we were talking about capitalization. Each student was giving me an example of a word that is always capitalized, easy words, such as Ethiopia, Dilla, their own name. I hesitated at Nasin Shaffi. Nasin was the slowest kid in the school; he scored zero on every quiz I gave and was teased by the other students. I every quiz I gave and was teased by the other students. I didn't want to embarrass him again. When I asked him for a proper noun, he stood up and mumbled something.

"What?" I said.

Nasin repeated what he had said, in clear, full tones: "Dag Hammerskjold."

On St. Patrick's Day I explained my Irish heritage to 7-A and the importance of the day. Abraham, the biggest troublemaker in the school, raised his hand. "We should go outside, madam, to celebrate your holiday."

"No, that's not necessary," I said, but the students were already moving towards the door.

"Yes, yes, good idea," they said.

Tsegay Mekonnen, the class monitor, stood at the door to stop them. "No," he said. "It is her holy day. We must have five minutes of silent prayer." Not what I had in mind, but they all went back to their seats and bowed their heads.

The first time I saw Tsegay in action, he was stepping across a desk in the back of my room with a switch in his hand to hit another boy who was talking out of turn. It was my first day at Atse Dawit School.

"Hey, stop that. What do you think you're doing?" I said.

"No, madam. Is okay. He is the monitor."

Tsegay stood against the back wall with his arms laced across his blue shirt watching me advance on him. "I am monitor," he said when I reached him.

"Who says you are monitor?" I asked. I was familiar with the monitor system of class discipline, didn't like it, and didn't want it in my classroom.

` Tsegay shrugged and the other students again confirmed that he was the class monitor. I said the monitor should be elected by the class and proceeded to explain the democratic process, the duties of the monitor (no switches allowed), the responsibilities of the students to each other, to the monitor, and to their teachers, and then took nominations from the floors. They elected Ayelu Hailu.

Because not everybody was able to start school when they were six years old, the age range of my seventh graders was twelve to twenty-two. Ayelu was a slight twelve-year-old, the smallest boy in the class, meek and overwhelmed by his sudden elevation to high office. The students snickered when I announced the election results. I insisted that they respect Ayelu, affirmed my confidence in him, and said that his word would be law regarding areas of discipline. Ayelu took a deep breath, realigned his shoulders, and strutted to the back of the room where he could keep an eye on everybody. I resumed the math lesson.

He lasted four days.

The second time around they elected Hamid. I was pleased. Most of the students had the chiseled features, slight frame, and red-brown skin of the highland Ethiopian, but Hamid's family had emigrated from the far west. He was an imposing figure, six feet tall and pure black. But his service as monitor was a day shorter than Ayelu's and I didn't understand why he was unsuccessful until later, when I heard him called the black one, and *shankalla* (slave).

I told 7-A that I was furious with them for electing two successive monitors whom they refused to respect.

"Tsegay is our monitor, madam," somebody said.

And so he was. He became an invaluable advisor for me, an inside operator. "Bekele is not sick, madam. He have woman." Or "Kebede hates Hamid. Better move him." When I remember my class now, Tsegay's handsome face is always in the middle of the back row, his eyes roving over the rows of students. By the end of the year I had convinced him to give up the switch, but I noticed faint lines in his forehead and a wariness in his eyes when he confronted certain students.

We had electricity from 6 p.m. to 12 p.m. most nights. I planned lessons and graded papers when the lights were on, but I felt no obligation to my students when the lights went out at midnight. I sat up with a book pressed flat against the table, reading by candlelight in the dark kitchen. The only noise was the occasional cough of a hyena passing in the street and the *sitz* of insects flying into the flame. I blew the specks of their parts out of the fold as I turned the pages. I savored each word of those delicious books. I also read *Time* cover to cover every week, including the sports and business sections; I read the listings of books published on the flyleaf of Penguin library editions; I read the small print of ads in the English-language *Ethiopian Herald,* a weekly newspaper.

I even read *The Fanny Farmer Cookbook* cover to cover. I knew nothing about cooking. I was raised by a mother who claimed that packaged foods were the most profound advance of the twentieth century. She relied heavily on frozen fish sticks, chicken pot pies, and canned asparagus. All her cookbooks had "Jiffy" in the title.

There was no processed food in Dilla. We could dependably buy only onions, bananas, and meat. Sometimes there was cabbage and carrots. Once there was eggplant. We could also get rice, but there were insects in it. You had to dump it on the table and pull the rice into a bowl in your lap while killing the bugs and pushing them off to the side. Salt and spices were measured into cones of old newspaper, weighed, and sold. The egg man delivered his tiny eggs wrapped in banana leaves, thirty for a dollar Ethi. We bought oatmeal, canned margarine, tuna fish, powdered milk, and tins of vegetables when we went to Addis Ababa. The tuna fish and tinned vegetables were so precious that we allowed ourselves to eat them only on special occasions. In the end, we left two cans of beets, one of green beans, and one of corn for the next Volunteers. We wrote them a long letter, introducing them to our town, our kids, and our canned vegetables.

There was only one female Ethiopian teacher at Atse Dawit School. I don't remember her name. Claudie and I

Once, before a staff meeting, in front of everybody, the Weizerite asked me how I expected to raise a family with such small breasts, so I didn't like her very much, but Claudie made friends with her. Claudie told her we wanted to learn to cook Ethiopian, so she came by one afternoon with eight newspaper cones of different spices and told us to grind each spice separately, then spread it in the sun to dry, then grind each once again, and separately, then spread it in the sun to dry, then grind it again, then dry it, then grind one more time. Then we were to mix it in such and such proportions, sauté the onions for two hours until all the water was out of them, then mix in the spices. "Meanwhile," she said and started chopping a kilo of mutton into cubes the size of her thumb nail. I stopped listening. My heritage of jiffy cooking made me inadequate to the task, but Claudie wrote it all down. We never cooked anything with the *Weizerite's* spices. Our last week in Dilla, we sifted the spices into *birillas,* the bulb-shaped glasses used for drinking honey *tej,* sealed them with wax, and took them home to America. They still line the top shelf of the highest cabinet in my kitchen.

One day Ato Mahari and Ato Hamare, the Amhara bankers in town, dropped by for tea and invited the four of us on a picnic.

"Terrific," I said. "Do you want us to bring something?"

"Yes, of course, you women will cook, but we will hunt first. We will get partridges and lesser kudu and have a picnic in the grand style," Ato Mahari said. Mahari and Hamare were as *ferenji* as we were in Dilla where the people were either Sidominia or Derasse. The two of them, the four of us, plus Ato Aberra, a big man on the Coffee Board, and Ato Bekele, the school superintendent, formed the middle class of Dilla. A handful of local landowners and Negussie and Mohammed, who owned bars, were the upper class. Mahari's and Hamare's wives were shy, elegant class. Mahari's and Hamare's wives were shy, elegant women who didn't eat with us when we were invited to their houses and they wouldn't be going with us on the grand picnic.

Claudie and I couldn't find a single reference to lesser kudu in *Fanny Farmer.* We approached Dick and Doug for help. They were sitting on their front porch with Tafesse, the third grade teacher who lived with them. Dick had just come back from a soccer game and had a towel wrapped around his head to soak up the sweat. Doug was reading. Tafesse was smoking a cigarette.

"They expect us to cook," I said. "You have to help us."

Dick rubbed his head with the towel. Tafesse stubbed out his cigarette and grinned. Doug looked up from his book.

"You're the best cook," Claudie said to Doug. "You cook the kudu."

"Can't," he said. "Would be insulting to Mahri and Hamare. We are guests in their country and must obey their customs."

"It is clearly woman's work," Dick said.

Even Tafesse laughed when I said, "Come on, you guys, this is serious."

They wouldn't help us, so Claudie and I concocted a salad that we loosely referred to as cole slaw, bought bread from Montenari's, and took the *Weizerite's* spices.

The day of the picnic Mahri did kill two of the tiny antelope known as lesser kudu. He skinned and bled them for roasting while Hamare built the fire and Claudie and I paced nervously.

"We've got these spices," I said, but Mahari roasted the delicate kudu parts without the spices and we had our grand picnic in a grove of flat-topped acacia trees under the watchful eyes of local Derasse children. Later Dick and Mahari played with their revolvers as if they were cap guns. In my pictures from that day, there is a series of shots of the two of them facing off with the guns in their pockets,

Western gunslinger style. Dick has a towel wrapped around his head and his hand on his hip, ready to draw: Mahari is doubled-over, laughing at the crazy American.

Even the most remote town in Ethiopia has one or two Italian men who married Ethiopian women after World War II and stayed on to bake bread or make pasta. In Dilla, Montenari ran a small bar and had the only bakery. There had been a second Italian in town, who ran the generator, but he died shortly before we arrived, so Montenari was alone. One Friday, Doug and I stopped at his bar just before midnight. The place was empty, he was ready to close, but he still had coffee, so he poured us some, and himself some, and he sat with us. He spoke no English and only a little Amharic, and we spoke no Italian, so the three of us sat there in silence, this old Italian and two young Americans, drinking espresso in the middle of Ethiopia. At midnight, the lights went out. Montenari held his hand up and shook his head, insisting that we stay. He brought candles and more coffee. We sat with him a while longer and listened to the hyenas who began their eerie whoops as soon as the electricity shut off.

When we finally left Montenari alone and walked back to our houses in the dark, Doug took my hand. "Yes," he said, "Paris is like this."

Ato Aberra, the Coffee Board man, loved to play cards with us, especially after we taught him Hearts. He was a born capitalist and never accepted the idea that in Hearts the *low* scorer wins—he was a twenty-five-point man. I ran into him at the bank one day, surrounded by huge boxes of money. Each box held $600 Ethi in five-cent pieces, 1,800 coins per box. Aberra explained that he was on his way out to buy coffee and the Derasse wouldn't accept paper money or any coin larger than a five-cent piece. "You can have any box you can carry away yourself," he said.

Bizunesh, the crazy woman, was usually the only beggar in Dilla. She'd smile sadly, with her head cocked to the side and her hand out when you passed her, but once she swooped at me, as if she were tackling me around the knees, and kissed my shoes. But other beggars appeared on holy days.

On St. Mikhel's day, the school and all businesses closed because there was a St. Mikhel's Church near Dilla. All the Coptic Christians in town congregated on the soccer field in front of the school. The priests, dressed in their brightest velvets, gathered at one end of the field surrounded by acolytes holding red, purple, and gold umbrellas over their holy heads and swinging incense burners in front of them. The town officials flanked them on the left. The teachers, with the four Peace Corps Volunteers in the front row, sat on the right. The speeches and invocations lasted two hours; most of the ceremony was in Ge'ez, the religious language of the Coptic Church. Only the priests knew exactly what was going on. After the speeches, we proceeded to the church. Everybody went: students, women with small children, farmers, bar owners, prostitutes, and the four *ferenjis*. It was a ten-kilometer walk, and beggars lined both sides of the roads and paths the whole way. The biggest concentration surrounded the gates to the church courtyard. Lepers without fingers or toes or with parts of their faces wasted away, men with elephantiasis (one or both of their legs swollen like a tree trunk), legless men, crazy women, emaciated women with children with distended bellies, women with open, oozing sores; the lame, the poor, the insane were all trotted out for the procession. Giving to the poor was part of every holy ritual.

We could get BBC, Voice of America, Radio Moscow, Radio Deutschville, and sometimes Radio Vatican in Dilla. Abraham interrupted my algebra class one day. "Why do you shoot Negroes in bars?" he said.

"And burn your cities?" someone else asked. They listened to the radio too.

Lester Maddox, the restaurateur who sold axe handles to keep African Americans out of his Pickwick Restaurant, was elected governor of my home state that November. Tsegay Mekonnen asked me about the new governor of Georgia and axe handles.

"The democratic process doesn't always work the way you think it ought to," I said.

Tsegay nodded. He already knew that.

I had a party for the seventy-five students in my homeroom the week before we left Dilla for good. I made popcorn and bought a stock of bananas for refreshments, but I was stumped when it came to entertainment. Music was out: Our radio reception was too poor and I had no record player. The house was small—two twelve-foot-by-twelve-foot rooms—but I thought the kids could mingle and talk, eat a banana, and extend the party out into the yard. But they wouldn't go outside. They filled one room, two and three deep, crushed against the four walls. I tried to engage them in conversation, but they were politely monosyllabic. I distributed the popcorn and organized Pin the Tail on the Donkey in the other room, but the easy laughter and conversation from the classroom were silenced by the solemnity of the occasion. The party in my house had made them mute.

Finally, Tsegay said, "Madam, can we dance?"

"Yes, of course. But where and to what music?" There was a square yard of open floor at best.

"Don't worry, miss." Tsegay issued instructions to several of the students, took Addiswork's scarf, and stepped to the center of the room. Yakob found an empty patch of wall and drummed the mud plaster with the fingers and heel of his hand. Tsegay began moving in small circles in the middle of the room. The girls sang. Bekele clapped his hands in counterpoint to Yakob's drumming. Tsegay moved faster, holding the scarf taut between his hands, over his head, behind his back, then dropping an end, following it. Everybody sang, punctuating their songs with shouts and ululations.

They were of different tribes, different religions, but they knew what to do. When Tsegay finished, Addiswork took her scarf and stepped to the center of the room. Everybody sang and drummed as she began to move. My party was a success.

On our last day, we got up early to take the first bus to Addis Ababa. When I opened the back door in the predawn light, to go to the outhouse, I discovered Tsegay, Hamid, Zeudi, Ayelu, Mulugetta, Nasin, and Zelalen waiting in the yard. Dozens of students had gathered in the dark so they wouldn't miss our departure. They hovered around our two houses as we packed. They trailed us down the dirt roads of Dilla for the last time. They insisted on carrying our things to the bus. Tsegay presented me with a basket his mother made. "So her name will be known in your country," he said. We got on the bus and waved until we couldn't see them anymore.

The road out of Dilla is a steep climb and the bus slows almost to a stop by the last switchback. There is a point where the whole town is as visible as a map—four parallel streets, up from the river, bisected by paths, with the school at the high end and the bus park where clumps of our kids still waved at the low end. The four of us craned towards the windows for a last look. "So this was Paris," Dick said softly.

"This was better," I said.

Kathleen Coskran (Ethiopia 1965-67) taught English and math in Dilla, Ethiopia, and spent two years in Kenya. Her book, *The High Price of Everything,* winner of a Minnesota Book Award in 1988, includes stories set in both Ethiopia and Kenya. She currently teaches fiction writing at Hamline University and at the University of Minnesota.

Nigeria, West Africa

The Rains Will Come

by Tony Zurlo

The brown savanna is cracked,
    as if the whole world
is dehydrating.
But the rains will come
as sure as the Cow Fulani
return in slow motion
with their Zeebu cattle,
while egrets ride the humps
and flap long white wings.
Other birds sit silently
in the knotty arthritic branches
of ageless baobab trees,
waiting for the rains.

The sun stretches on the horizon
for a moment of rest
before dropping to the other side.
The globe spreads shades
of purple, rose, and yellow
across the savanna.

In the distance, shifting shadows
animate still life paintings of
farmers behind plows,
donkeys loaded with wood,
a thatched lean-to with women
selling kola nuts and smoked fish,
and naked children splashing in a puddle.

Tony Zurlo (Nigeria 1965-66) has published poetry, reviews and fiction and is the author of several books on Asia. He currently lives in Fort Worth, Texas.

Sierra Leone, West Africa

An African Beggar

by Margaret Przywara

I would like to tell a little story that symbolizes what the Peace Corps meant to me.

My story takes place in Freetown, Sierra Leone. Freetown is a modern city surrounded by beautiful mountains and golden beaches, but my story is about a beggar and me and takes place on the busy streets of the city.

The beggar, whose name I never knew, had a horrible case of leprosy. The fingers were almost all eaten away, and he could walk only with the help of a cane. His clothes were ragged, and he wore no shoes, and daily I would see him limping through the busy streets of Freetown begging for money. People threw money on the ground as the man approached. No one, naturally, wanted to get too close to a leper with such obvious disfigurement.

After weeks of trying to beg money from me without success, he blocked my way one morning and demanded that I give him money. I threw a few pennies onto the ground and rushed away, but I knew at once that I could not continue to give him money. I hadn't come to Freetown to give money to beggars. I had joined the Peace Corps to help another country and learn another culture.

That day I asked a Sierra Leonian woman, to whom I was teaching secretarial skills, what I should do about the beggar.

"He doesn't really want your money," she replied matter of factly.

"Doesn't want it?" I asked. "He demands it!"

"This man eats well. I see him at every store in town and the storekeepers throw him food. This man wants something more from you," she said with a shy smile and a sideward glance at me. "This man wants your respect."

I thought about what she said that night and the next day when the beggar came up to me, I shook my head no when he demanded his pennies. He started carrying on and yelling things in his own tribal language, but I just kept shaking my head with my hands folded in front of me. It would have been easy to reach into my bag for three or four pennies, but I knew I could not give in. Suddenly, the Freetown skies seemed to open and it began to pour. I raised my umbrella and turned to walk away. The beggar had grown quiet as the heavy, tropical rain beat down on him. I stopped walking and turned and walked back to him.

"Stand under my umbrella until the rain passes," I told him. He gave me a surprised look but remained under the umbrella. We never spoke a word for the few minutes it continued to rain and when the sun reappeared, I closed my umbrella, smiled, and waved good-bye.

The following day I saw him again. This time, instead of demanding money from me, he smiled and waved and continued limping down the street. We had both gained something that day: respect for each other.

Maybe this story seems insignificant to you. I didn't change the world. I didn't build skyscrapers and I didn't end world hunger. But maybe, just maybe, that beggar and all the other African lives I touched during my two years there

may remember me as I can, clearly and fondly, remember
them.

Margaret Przywara (Nigeria & Sierra Leone 1968-70) was a Peace
Corps secretary and delivered this address at the the Journals of Peace, a
24-hour vigil of readings by Returned Peace Corps Volunteers held in the
Capitol Rotunda in 1988 to mark twenty-five years since the death of John
F. Kennedy.

Togo, West Africa

A Clash of Cultures

by Tom Peirce

In Togo, as a new Volunteer, I learned the hard way what it means to understand, to communicate, in another culture. Eager to do something constructive, but absent an understanding of local conditions, I naively initiated the planting of two mango tree nurseries. Both were subsequently eaten by wandering goats; I later learned that the village elder I was planting with did not warn me to build an anti-goat fence since he believed that I wanted him to participate in the work but that I would then deviously sell the trees for my own profit. Undiscouraged, I soon decided, after a casual conversation with my local French teacher, that I'd found a new opportunity to meet the goals of my assigned program in Cooperatives and Development.

He explained that in the Kara region weaving is a declining art form, restricted by a local market, the influx of western clothing, and a lack of start-up capital. This left most weavers unable to use their skills to generate income. Determined to help, I asked my teacher to assist in arranging a series of meetings with local weavers. Three months of planning followed where the teacher, myself, and a group of eleven women weavers held meeting after meeting to discuss marketing, production, and capital needs. Finally, it seemed that an ideal project was about to be launched in the form of a weaving cooperative.

My enthusiasm was replaced by disbelief when I returned from a short vacation and found that all of the women had quit the co-op. It took two weeks to find out that my teacher, speaking Kabayé and then translating responses in French to me, had told the women that the cooperative must rent his workspace. They explained that they had been too scared to publicly refuse and that, furthermore, the elected president of the cooperative had offered free use of her workplace, but that this had not been translated during our meetings. I had acquiesced to my teacher's plan by giving the translating power to a man in an environment where authority is hierarchically defined by men and rarely challenged openly. I also had not given the women enough credit. Most of them spoke French perfectly well, but were initially too shy to use it. Eventually, once the women had control of the meetings, they reorganized the co-op without my teacher's involvement and participated in learning management skills with the objective of enhancing their control over business decisions.

When my two years came to an end, I was reasonably optimistic about the co-op's future. I also found that I was leaving behind numerous friends. It was hard not to get choked up as I drove away on my motorcycle from my last meeting and saw in my mirror the group president running behind, waving good-bye, and crying. Four years later, I still receive letters from the original president and secretary, with photos of their latest designs. Each time I receive a letter from Madame Tchedre or Madam Kao, I realize how important my experience was towards opening my mind to the world, neutralizing cultural ignorance and naiveté.

As personal as my experience was, when I read about the experiences of other returned Volunteers I realized that most of us found an awakening within ourselves and returned with a new perspective on our world. Our world. It is no longer possible for me to think of the world in the abstract geopolitical terms my academic career had taught. Rather, I am aware of the complex maze of cultures and the challenge of bridging them together. Yet, increasingly, foreign and domestic attitudes towards alien cultures seem to fall into one of two extremes. At one end is a perspective that denies that cultural differences matter, contending that the basic worldview of all people is the same. This school of thought, that of the politically correct, has the potential to create endless misunderstandings and confusion. Even more damaging is the other extreme, where xenophobes spew virulent strains of nationalism, heralding an emerging clash of cultures. Xenophobes gain support as they incite conflict based on cultural issues and advocate battle against *The Other* as defense of their own souls.

The value of the intercultural experience is that it enables a middle ground to evolve between these two poles. It develops both an intellectual understanding that social, economic, and institutional forces can converge to create profound cultural differences and an emotional understanding that, in the end, we all share a common humanity. The challenge of our time is to move individuals to this middle ground, substituting misunderstanding and fear based on cultural ignorance with constructive material and spiritual progress.

Tom Peirce (Togo 1988-90) is Peace Corps' Historian. He received his B.A. in international relations from Tufts University and is completing his M.A. in political science at George Washington University.

Micronesia, Pacific

Hearts and Minds

by P. F. Kluge

It was hearts-and-minds time in the Pacific [in the late 1960s] and that is how the Peace Corps came to paradise, with a saturation program designed to show what the Peace Corps could do when the host-country government was basically American. "The Peace Corps intends to alter substantially in a relatively short period of time, say three to five years, the [U.S. government's] twenty-year record of neglect and dismal achievement," one memo crowed. That, it turned out, was a mistake. The Peace Corps oversold itself enormously, with a Stalingrad of good intentions, over 900 Volunteers at one point. If the same ratio went to India, someone joked, there would be no young people left in the United States. What the arithmetic really worked out to, I learned later, was that if the same ratio went to India, there'd be five million Peace Corps Volunteers there. In its nonaligned wisdom, India satisfied itself with sixty-five of America's finest.

My billet was in the Northern Marianas on Saipan, headquarters of the Trust Territory government, an office right down the hall from the high commissioner. Capital Hill, the place was called, although it was Mount

Tagpouchau on maps and Mount Olympus to the locals. It commanded a view of the island, the invasion beaches on the west side, Japanese bunkers, spiked and gutted, pointing out toward rusting American tanks and landing craft. On the south were airstrips, Kobler and Isley, and, across the three-mile strait, Tinian Island, and the airstrips that the *Enola Gay* took off from, Hiroshima bound. Saipan's west side was rocky, a moonscape of limestone cliffs that climbed toward the north end of the island, Marpi District. That's where the World War II fighting ended, with mass suicides off Suicide and Banzai cliffs. It was still an eerie, death-haunted place.

I was a "high-caste" Volunteer, editing a quarterly magazine, the *Micronesian Reporter*, traveling at will—and on per diem—through a swatch of islands that were going to be my personal Yoknapatawha. I saw the Marshall Islands, palm-fringed atolls traumatized by nuclear testing at Bikini and Eniwetok. I hiked the rain forests of Ponape, drank in the famously squalid bar of the Truk Trading Company. When Lee Marvin came, scouting locations for something that was later called *Hell in the Pacific*, I accompanied him on a beery tour of Saipan, searching out the place where he'd been wounded, shot in the ass he claimed, twenty-five years before. On Tinian, I could find my way down baking empty runways to the bomb pits where they'd loaded the *Enola Gay*. On Yap, I visited the village of Rull, where topless locals had been known to throw stones at Japanese tourists. And then there was Palau, where an air of conspiracy, ambition, and sensuality hit you the minute you stepped off the plane. A steamy, movie set of a place, cameras ready, actors clamoring, everything in place, and its script still waiting to be written.

The best part of the *Micronesian Reporter*—and the only way of getting some island voices in the magazine—was a long front-of-book interview section, much like *Playboy's*. Lots of head shots. I was looking for a lively Micronesian voice. So many of them said little, or clowned, or catered to their questioner, or kept their best words for closing time in bars, with Jim Reeves on the jukebox and bottles breaking out in the parking lot. Someone recommended Salii, a young Palauan who'd graduated from the University of Hawaii, spent some time back in Palau, and was now doing something or other in the Trust Territory personnel office.

Salii was a dark man of medium height with the sort of chunky body you could tell was going to bother him someday. His voice, low and hoarse, had some of the Brooklynisms he'd picked up from Jesuit priests; he'd talk about how things were "gonna" be. His face was what you watched. No inscrutability, no island coyness here. His frown was the essence of worry, his glare was all-out contempt, and his smile, when it broke through, was every good joke.

The interview was no barn burner. He offered sensible, temperate criticism of a government that wasn't used to hearing it, at least not in print and not from Micronesians who, by God, worked at headquarters! What people noticed was Salii's assumption—not insistence, but assumption—that Micronesians had the right to decide what became of this trusteeship, whose days were numbered. The islands belonged to them, not to the U.S. or the U.N., and so would the government. It wasn't a radical argument, it wasn't made in anger. Sovereignty, self-determination, self-government: Surely there was nothing dangerous in all this, nothing that Americans could fail to understand. No? Then let's get on with it! Sooner or later, Americans were going to have to talk about the future of these islands. They were going to have to acknowledge that the people they administered—their wards—had the right to say yes or no: to independence, to territorial status, to military bases and missile test sites. That was what Salii insisted upon, a role for the islanders. A role for himself. When the game started, he was going to be there.

Salii was brisk and businesslike. So was I. It wasn't

until later I realized that we were destined to be friends.
After my Peace Corps stint ended, Salii called me to the
Congress of Micronesia, where he'd become a senator from
Palau. I hadn't seen much of him since the interview appeared, though I was aware he'd gotten some copies for use
in a political campaign back home. He wasn't much for
easy socializing. You heard from him when he wanted
something. Maybe this was Palauan opportunism. Or some
combination of arrogance and shyness. An awkwardness
with friendship. I suspect this, because I sensed the same
thing in myself.

The old Congress of Micronesia—which was torched a
few years later, when the Trust Territory was splitting up—
was a couple of military-surplus buildings perched on a
limestone crag above the upper-crust housing area on
Capital Hill. Low on money, low on power, high on noise-
making, it drew most of its members from the Micronesians
who worked for the Trust Territory government. What pleasure they took in calling their bosses into hearings, grilling
them about pay scales, promotions, waste! This gave
Congress the air of one of those youth-takeover days in
which bright-eyed students play at being mayors and city
councilmen. Still, something was up and Salii was right in
the middle of it. He headed the Future Political Status
Commission. Everybody granted that the U.S. trusteeship
would have to end someday, but no one knew when, or how,
or what would follow it. Annexation by the United States, a
territory like Guam, just to the south, or like American
Samoa? Commonwealth, like Puerto Rico? Statehood?
Independence?

Salii and the other members had traveled from Samoa
to the Virgin Islands, taking notes that he half heartedly suggested I might want to read sometime. But what was needed
now, he said, was a short statement, sexy and eloquent, a
way of capturing the United States' attention. A statement
of what?

He laid it out for me, in about five minutes, and then he

walked away, leaving me with a naked yellow legal pad. He liked doing that, I later learned. Wham, bam, thank you ma'am, the destiny of Micronesia. Take all the time you need, he indicated. He made it sound like a challenge. Stay with me if you can, I'll be moving fast on this one, he implied. I stayed with him for the next twenty years, in a relationship that exhilarated me at times, depressed me at others. I wondered about it. In everything else I wrote— books, scripts, magazine articles—I worked in a measured, disciplined way, three pages a day or five, pacing myself, planning for the long haul, realizing that each day's increment was a fraction of the total manuscript I aimed for. Discipline, not inspiration, was what counted. Stamina. I watched my writing the way I watched my drinking, not wanting to wake up in a strange place, hung over, wondering what happened the night before. Salii was the one exception. Something clicked between us. For him I went all out, drained the bottle, closed the bar, finished the document he wanted in one sitting, service ace, never worrying about the number of words, or pages, or hours.

In fact, it took about an hour, words and music, and it was his doing as much as mine, the Statement of Intent, which later was compared to the Declaration of Independence and Africa's Lusaka Manifesto. There was a dash of history, conquest upon conquest, war after war. The early colonizing powers. Then a glance at the U.S. record in Micronesia, with some pointed references to the U.N. trusteeship agreement, which obliged the United States to offer "self-government or independence." Then, the assertion that the islands belonged to Micronesians, after all, and so did the responsibility for governing them. The choice was theirs.   And what they chose was...tricky. The Micronesians said they'd like to negotiate a relationship of "free association" with the United States. The islanders would write their constitution, control their lands, run their government, and have the right to end their relationship with America, the right—you could almost see the

Pentagon swallowing hard—to secede. The United States would be granted defense rights in exchange for an unspecified amount of money. And, if free association didn't work out, the Micronesians would go for the only other worthy alternative: outright independence.

Never before, never since, have I seen anything I'd written so please a reader. A secret weapon, a manifesto! But it wasn't what the Statement of Intent said. Salii had left lots of crucial questions undecided. The free association he talked about was a compromise between heart and head; between the desire for independence and the realities of a tiny, sluggish, neo-colonial economy. There was no way of knowing what free association would amount to or where it would lead. Was it an end in itself or was it a temporary status, something that might lead toward eventual independence or gravitate, instead, toward closer ties with the United States? Free association was vague, open-ended, subject to later change. It wasn't the end of the game, just the beginning.

Salii seemed to feel that the negotiations would be brisk, straightforward, quid pro quo. Smart men could always reach an agreement and he was smart. I had my doubts. But the important thing was that the islanders were taking the initiative. They weren't going to let the decision be made in Washington. Here they were, taking on the Americans. That was the drama of it. And I was coming along. Salii asked me to stick around a few months, to join him and some other congressmen on a tour of the districts, holding village meetings, trumpeting the Statement of Intent. Starting, he said, in Palau. I could sense the excitement; we were building a nation, or something.

The boat rides, the village arrivals, the feasts and meetings; the nights in men's houses and municipal dispensaries, joking and bullshitting and dreaming: Those next weeks stayed with me for years.

It wasn't all fun. The village meetings were difficult. People pleaded ignorance, prayed for caution, asked for time. They wanted independence. They worried about money. They feared change. The Trust Territory government wasn't great but it was bearable. Getting closer to the Americans was scary; moving farther away from them was scarier.

Every now and then, I found myself in the middle of a special moment. Often, Salii provided it. There was an afternoon in Truk, on the island of Tol. Sweaty and tired, Salii got up to wrangle with a question that had no answer: the prospect of military presence in the islands. Would his proposed free association change things?

"If the United States wants to pull out of Okinawa tomorrow and come to Tol, we have no choice," he began. "I'm old enough to remember the last war and I know what war means and I have spoken out against their coming. This proposal of ours doesn't necessarily mean they can't come in. It gives us a voice in the matter. Now, we can't say *anything* about it. Do you want to continue under the current system or change it?"

While he paused to have his words turned into Trukese, I glanced around the room: a hundred men inside a meeting house, dirt floored, thatch roofed, open at the sides. Outside, dozens more were underneath the eaves, in the shade. On a nearby hillside, some old men and women sat underneath a mango tree. Farther uphill, a woman knelt by a stream, pounding wash against a slab of rock. Salii resumed.

"We have seen how the military worked in Kwajalein and Eniwetok and Bikini. They used their legal power to acquire land with nominal payment. If we continue the trusteeship system as it is today, this is the kind of situation we will have to face. Now, under our proposal, we are saying that if the United States wants to use some land, they will come to the government of Micronesia and ask where they can put bases and airstrips. And the government will designate islands and areas that can be used and arrange for compensation. We would do this under the proposed free association. We cannot do this today."

Another pause for translation. Why hadn't he given a simpler answer, I wondered, something less hedged. Now the United States can do what it wants. We want to limit their power. But we can't get rid of it completely. The other guys often clowned and joked when they spoke. Salii soliloquized. He wasn't speaking to the crowd, I realized. He was talking to himself, thinking out loud.

"This is a very important and difficult question, and I'm sure we're not giving very satisfactory answers. But we have agonized over these questions for the past two years. As we look over our history, wars have always been a part of us. We are situated between two huge masses of land, and great powers cross through us on their way to fight. Knowing human nature, we will have to accept the military in our lives and learn to live with them."

I don't know if what he said pleased Salii. I don't know whether he believed it, or half believed it, or believed half of it, then or later. I doubt that more than a handful of his listeners grasped the balances and compromises he set out for them. I was his best audience, I guess. And what startled me was hearing him, there, then, weighing the hardest of questions in a village meeting house, with a sunken Japanese fleet in the lagoon and rusted artillery pieces still pointing out of hillside caves. That, I thought, was something.

I never cared as much about politics in Los Angeles or New York as I did there, at the end of the world, and never met a more congenial bunch of leaders. Splendid fellows, I thought, the first generation of American-educated politicians, returning home determined to hold the United States to its word. No military garrison state here, no indian reservation either. These were nation builders. San Martins and Bolivars, Paines and Washingtons, and my pleasure, as I got to know them, was to wonder who was who. The burly Yapese, John Mangefel, chewing betelnut and citing Chaucer, what role would he play? Or Luke Tman, a Palauan-Japanese, raised in Yap, mixing the nearly scholastic mind of a chess player and parliamentarian with the looks of a matinee idol? And Amata Kabua, courtly mandarin boss of the Marshall Islands, Bailey Olter, loud and buoyant, a connoisseur of dredges and backhoes, an earthmoving, shit-kicking man. From Truk there came Tosiwo Nakayama, already an advocate of independence, a quiet man whom I suspect didn't trust me, or maybe it was that he didn't know me, which made his occasional confidences feel like medals. But Salii was at the heart of it all.

I had a better sense of him now. I saw how strengths could shade into weaknesses. Drive and urgency, for instance, imploded into plain restlessness, never more evident than when he was in Palau. He lacked patience, what the Germans called *Sitzfleish*. He was anxious to take off, go somewhere, confront and flurry, when he'd have been better off letting things ripen, letting others come to him. There was more. As impressed as I was by Salii's drive, I sometimes wondered what his ends were, whether he looked beyond the negotiations that were just starting. Did he have an idea what victory was? Could he enjoy it? How did he want things to be really? I saw that he was moody and impulsive, I wondered if he were a stayer, a ten-round fighter. Still, he was my pick for George Washington. Once, just before I left, he thanked me for what I'd done, the statements and speeches and newspaper accounts.

"We won't forget you," Salii said, while we drove around Koror one morning. "Hell," I responded, prematurely cynical. "Who remembers the name of Paul Revere's horse?"

"Paul Revere did," he replied.

Postscript: In January 1981, Palau became a republic. When they selected their first president, the Palauans bypassed the mercurial, high-flying Salii and settled on a man of the people, a gentler sort, one of their own. A dark, steady, competent man, Haruo Remeliik had been an assistant district administrator in the old Trust Territory days. There'd been too many leaders lately, too many battles revolving around the constitution and the compact. Now they wanted someone calm and likable. So Palau chose its George Washington. And then proceeded to destroy him.

In late June 1985, old women looked up, looked south, and shuddered at what they called a matted sky, full of closely woven clouds, like the funeral mats placed around a fresh grave. Someone high, someone from the south, someone was doomed to die. Late on the night of June 20, Peleliu-born Haruo Remeliik was met outside his home on Koror's topside ridge. Shot four times, the dead president rolled down a slope at the side of his driveway.

Palau bristled with intricate, elegant theories involving drugs, a power plant, bribes, spies, hit men. But the murder of Palau's first elected president was unsolved.

No unequivocal acts in a place like Palau. Three men were later arrested, convicted, then released on appeal.

In February 1986 I stopped in Palau. My arrival coincided with a ceremony. I drove up to a knoll that overlooks Koror, parked at the side of the road, joined a crowd of pedestrians walking up to the grounds of the Palau Museum. On the lawn, they were unveiling a statue of the murdered Remeliik. His genial, stoic face sat atop a pedestal, which carried a line from one of his speeches, something about unity and pride. There were speeches that sweltering morning, and prayers, and at the end of the ceremony a black sedan pulled out onto the driveway and stopped as it came to where I stood. The tinted window rolled down and there behind it sat Palau's second elected president, my old friend Lazarus Salii.

P.F. Kluge (Micronesia 1967-69) is the author of four novels and two works of non-fiction. A *Life* magazine story that he wrote was used as the basis of the film, *Dog Day Afternoon*. His novel, *Eddie and the Cruisers*, was also made into a movie. In 1988, his book, *The Edge of Paradise: America in Micronesia* won the Paul Cowan Prize given by *RPCV Writers & Readers*. His most recent book, *Alma Mater: A College Homecoming*, was published in 1993.

Saint Kit, West Indies

The Mending Fields

by Bob Shacochis

I was assigned to the Island of Saint Kit in the West Indies. Once on an inter-island plane I sat across the aisle from one of my new colleagues, an unfriendly, over-serious young woman. She was twenty-four, twenty-five... we were all twenty-four, twenty-five. I didn't know her much or like her. As the plane banked over the island, she pressed against the window, staring down at the landscape. I couldn't see much of her face, just enough really to recognize an expression of pain. Below us spread an endless manicured lawn, bright green and lush of sugarcane, the island's main source of income. Each field planted carefully to control erosion. Until that year Saint Kit's precious volcanic soil had been bleeding into the sea; somehow they had resolved the problem. The crop was now being tilled in harmony with the roll and tuck of the land and the island had taken a step to reclaiming its future. The woman peered out her window until the island was lost on the blue horizon. And then she turned forward in her seat and wept until she had soaked the front of her blouse. "Good Lord," I thought, "what's with her?" I found out later from another Volunteer: Two years ago, having just arrived on the island, she had been assaulted as she walked to her house. Not content to rape her, a pair of men had beaten her so severely she was sent back to the States to be hospitalized. Recovering, she had made the choice to return. She believed she could be of use on Saint Kit so she went back to coordinate the team responsible for improving the way sugarcane was cultivated. The day I flew with her was the first time she had taken a look at her handiwork from the illuminating vantage of the air. The cane fields were beautiful, perfect: they were a triumph, they were courage, and they were love.

Bob Shacochis (Eastern Caribbean 1975-76) is the author of two collections of stories, *Easy in the Islands,* winner of the 1985 American Book Award, and *The Next New World.* He also published a novel, *Swimming In The Volcano,* and *Domesticity A Gastronomic Interpreation of Love,* a collection of his GQ columns. Shacochis lives in Florida and is a contributing editor to both *Outside* Magazine and *Harper's.* In 1994, his book, *Swimming In the Volcano,* won the Maria Thomas Fiction Award given by *RPCV Writers & Readers.*

Niger, West Africa

Mariama

by Susan Rich

Late afternoons when Mariama held court
in our shared and barren yard
I would pick a favorite for her
from among the motorcycles
and second-hand Citroens
imagine interviewing the assorted suitors
at least to ease the traffic jam
the spectacle outside our house.

I'd wonder what she had
to make men want to charm her so
wait under the eyes of a prickly sun
flies climbing inside their collars
like old age sneaking up close.

Was it the sincere disinterest
with which she greeted each one
obese or debonair, rich or rather

less poor? Sometimes friends
who came to visit me
would turn and go to Mariama first
sanu, sanu—how are you? I'd hear them say
before the knock came at my door.

What *magani,* what potion did this adolescent hold
to inspire men's overheated dedication,
their ankles creaking as they shifted
their feet in line. Mariama told me once
her father was afraid that she was getting old
and demanded that she choose a bridegroom soon.

After all, she said, *he's the one
that gets my bride price: twenty goats
and a Sony stereo. It's a bargain,*
she spit her words
across the yard *and they all know it.*
Later when Zarma the cat was killed
cut into bite size pieces
we had the only other conversation
in all the time we lived together.

*Sai hankuri, sai hankuri,
have patience, have patience*
was her advice.
This she repeated like religious vows
a prayer that someday
the right answer would come.

Susan Rich (Niger 1984-86) was an English teacher in Zinder, Niger. Her
poems have appeared in the *Christian Science Monitor, The Massachusetts
Review, Southern Poetry Review* and *Passages North.* She is completing
her first book of poems, *In the Language of Maps* and holds degrees in
English from Harvard University and the University of Massachusetts. She
currently teaches creative writing at the Univeristy of Oregon.

Washington, D.C.

At Home In The World

by Bill Moyers

Sometimes the soundtrack of memories deep in my mind begins on its own to play back the Sixties with the echoes intercut to the incongruities of those years.

I hear the sounds of crowds cheering and cities burning; of laughing children and weeping widows; of nightrides, nightmares, and napalm; of falling barriers and new beginnings and animosities as old as Cain and Abel.

I hear the summons that opened the decade—"Let the word go forth"—and I hear the melancholy lament that closed it. "The stone was at the bottom of the hill," wrote one young man who had given his heart to three fallen heroes: "The stone was at the bottom of the hill, and we were alone."

But something survived those years that bullets could not stop. An idea survived, embodied in the Peace Corps Volunteers who are now 125,000 strong and still coming. This idea survived the flawed stewardship of those of us who were its first and amateur custodians. And it survives today notwithstanding the disarray, moral incoherence, and spiritual vagrancy of this present age. Because it survives, this is less a eulogy than a testimony to the power of the idea.

Of the private man John Kennedy I knew little. I saw him rarely. Once, when the 1960 campaign was over and he was ending a post-election visit to the LBJ Ranch, he pulled me over into a corner to urge me to abandon my plans for graduate work at the University of Texas and to come to Washington as part of the New Frontier. I told him that I had already signed up to teach at a Baptist school in Texas while pursuing my doctorate. Anyway, I said, "You're going to have to call on the whole faculty at Harvard. You don't need a graduate of Southwestern Baptist Theological Seminary." In mock surprise he said, "Didn't you know that the first president of Harvard was a Baptist? You'll be right at home."

And so I was.

So I remember John Kennedy not so much for what he was or what he wasn't but for what he empowered in me. We all edit history to give some form to the puzzle of our lives, and I cherish the memory of him for awakening me to a different story for myself. He placed my life in a larger narrative than I could ever have written. One test of a leader is knowing, as John Stuart Mill put it, that "the worth of the state, in the long run, is the worth of the individuals composing it." Preserving civilization is the work not of some miracle-working, superhuman personality but of each one of us. The best leaders don't expect us just to pay our taxes and abdicate, they sign us up for civic duty and insist we sharpen our skills as citizens. Furthermore, to the extent that we are saved each day from the savage heart still alive within each of us, we are saved by grace—singular grace: the touch of a warming spirit, an outstretched hand, a spirit opened to others, a life generously shared.

Public figures either make us feel virtuous about retreating into the snuggeries of self or they challenge us to act beyond our obvious capacities. America is always up for grabs, can always go either way. The same culture that produced the Ku Klux Klan, Lee Harvey Oswald, and the Jonestown massacre also produced Martin Luther King, Archibald MacLeish, and the Marshall Plan.

A desperate and alienated young man told me in 1970, after riots had torn his campus and town: "I'm just as good as I am bad. I think all of us are. But nobody's speaking to the good in me." In his public voice John Kennedy spoke to my generation of service and sharing; he called us to careers of discovery through lives open to others.

Henry David Thoreau said, "I love a broad margin to my life." Most of us do but seldom achieve it. By stoking our imagination, John Kennedy opened us to broad margins. The theologian Karl Barth was five years old when he first heard the music of Mozart. It would delight him all his life. In 1955 Barth addressed a letter to the long-deceased Mozart, thanking him for all the pleasure of the music—all the pleasure and discovery. "With an ear open to your musical dialectic," wrote Barth, "one can be young and become old, can work and rest, be content and sad; in short, one can live."

The music of discovery. It was for us not a trumpet but a bell, sounding in countless individual hearts that one clear note that said: "You matter. You can signify. You can make a difference." Romantic? Yes, there was romance to it. But we were not then so callous toward romance. The best Volunteers waged hand-to-hand combat with cynicism, and won. They kept winning, until today the Peace Corps has earned a reputation (to quote the *Washington Post*) as one of the world's most effective grassroots development organizations.

The idea was around. It was in the air. General James M. Gavin, the wartime hero, had called for a peacetime volunteer force to be started as an alternative to military service. Senator Hubert Humphrey was preparing legislation for a youth corps. Congressman Henry Reuss and Senator Richard Neuberger of Oregon had cosponsored a Point Four Youth Corps. But it took a President to embody the idea, for the word to be made flesh. The Talmud tells us that "in every age there comes a time when leadership suddenly comes forth to meet the needs of the hour. And so, there is no man who does not find his time, and there is no hour that does not have its leader." Perhaps. But the wait can sometimes seem interminable, and we may miss the leader if the hour is late or we are weary and do not hear the music. John Kennedy was right on time with his idea. And we responded: Catholics, Christian Fundamentalists, Jews, blacks, whites, from every part of the country, from all economic levels, from various and sundry backgrounds: skiers, mountain climbers, big-game hunters, preachers, journalists, prize fighters, football players, polo players, enough lawyers to staff an entire firm, and enough Ph.D.s for a liberal arts college.

What was the idea that summoned us? Out of my own Peace Corps experience came a small gift from Albert Schweitzer, a framed and autographed picture which to this day reminds me of Schweitzer's belief in "the affirmation of life." He defined this as "the spiritual act by which we cease to live unreflectively." It was said that the urge to join the Peace Corps was passion alone. Not so. Men and women, whatever their age, looked their lives over and chose to affirm. To affirm is the thing. And so they have—in quiet, self-effacing perseverance.

They come—these men and women—from a vein in American life as idealistic as the Declaration and as gritty as the Constitution. I was reminded of this the other day when I interviewed the octogenarian dean of American historians, Henry Steele Commager. Reviewing the critical chapters of our story, he said that great things were done by the generation that won independence and then formed our government. Great things were accomplished by the generation that saved the union and rid it of slavery. Great things were won by the generation that defeated the fascists of Europe and warlords of Japan and then organized the peace that followed. And—said Dr. Commager—there are *still* great things to be won...here at home and in the world.

So there are. But if we are to reckon with the growing concentration and privilege of power; if from the lonely retreats of our separate realities we are to create a new consensus of shared values; if we are to exorcise the lingering poison of racism, reduce the extremes of poverty and wealth, and overcome the ignorance of our heritage, history, and world; if we are to find a sense of life's wholeness and the holiness in one another; then from this deep vein which gave rise to the Peace Corps must come our power and light.

The idea? Herman Melville got it right. We Americans are not a narrow tribe of men. We are not a nation so much as a world. And these Volunteers have shown us how to be at home in the world.

Listen to writer Michael Ventura: "The dream we must seek to realize, the new human project, is not 'security,' which is impossible to achieve on the planet Earth in the latter half of the Twentieth century. It is not 'happiness,' by which we generally mean nothing but giddy forgetfulness about the danger of all our lives together. It is not 'self-realization,' by which people usually mean a separate peace. There is no separate peace...Technology has married us all to each other, has made us one people on one planet and until we are more courageous about this new marriage—our selves all intertwined—there will be no peace and the destination of any of us will be unknown. How far can we go together—men and women, black, brown, yellow, white, young and old? We will go as far as we can because we must go wherever it is we are going *together.* There is no such thing as going alone. Given the dreams and doings of our psyches, given the nature of our world, there is no such thing as *being* alone. If you are the only one in the room it is still a crowded room. But we are all together on this planet, you, me, us; inner, outer, together, and we're called to affirm our marriage vows. Our project, the new human task, is to learn how to consummate, how to sustain, how to enjoy this most human marriage—all parts, all of us."

America has a rendezvous it has scarcely imagined with what my late friend Joseph Campbell called "a mighty multicultural future." But we are not alone and the stone is not at the bottom of the hill. We have guides—125,000 Volunteers who have advanced the trip. They have been to where our country is going. Out there in the world, as John F. Kennedy might say, is truly the new frontier.

Bill Moyers (Peace Corps Staff/Washington, D.C. 1991-93) was an associate director and deputy director of the Peace Corps. He then became special assistant to President Lyndon B. Johnson. He left the government in 1967 for a career in journalism. This speech was delivered November 22, 1988, at a commemorative service in St. Matthew's Cathedral, Washington, D.C., to mark the twenty-fifth anniversary of the death of President John F. Kennedy.

Washington, D.C.

But No Postcards

by John Coyne

In October of 1960 when John F. Kennedy was campaigning for the presidency, he spoke after midnight on the campus of the University of Michigan and mentioned the idea of a Peace Corps. I was one of the first students to be swept up by his challenge to go to Asia, Africa, and Latin America and contribute part of our lives to our country.

I had never thought of leaving my country before. I would never have thought of leaving my state. Now I wanted to be part of the New Frontier. I wanted to do something for my country.

In the summer of '62, I went to Washington to train with the first group of Volunteers to Ethiopia. Towards the end of training we went to meet President Kennedy in the Rose Garden.

After a few words of welcome, he stepped down to shake hands and wish us well. And as he turned to leave he stopped and asked us to write, to tell him how it was going. And then he grinned and added, "But no postcards," referring to the famous postcard sent to a friend at home by a woman Volunteer in Nigeria in 1961. It was a postcard that spoke honestly about conditions in Africa and almost brought an end to the Peace Corps before Volunteers had a chance to prove their worth. Kennedy's postcard reference showed not only his ironic wit, but also his full awareness of what his new initiative, the Peace Corps, was doing around the world.

Those of us who left the White House lawn and went into Africa are older now than Kennedy was on that summer afternoon. Time and tragedy have touched us all. But fate has an odd way of balancing the scales.

The Peace Corps was not considered the bold new stroke of the New Frontier. Yet it is the Peace Corps that is the shining memory of those thousand days of Camelot.

Our service overseas was often silent and often went unheralded. Some of the bridges we built did not stand, a few of the schools where we taught are now closed, and many of the people we organized did not stay together. We were seldom as successful as we had hoped.

But the Peace Corps took us out of America and taught us to be citizens of the world. Because of the Peace Corps, all of us are forever changed.

And we were not the only ones changed.

In the mountains of Ethiopia after John F. Kennedy's death I stopped my Land Rover to pick up an old man and give him a lift across the high plateau. On the side door he read the Peace Corps name, written in Amharic script as *Yesalaam Guad*. It meant Messenger of Peace.

I nodded and told him, yes, *Yesalaam Guad*. Kennedy's Peace Corps. He asked me then if I had known President Kennedy, and I told him how I had once shaken his hand on the White House lawn.

For a moment he looked out across the flat brown land at the distant acacia trees and small tukul villages we were passing, and then he grinned and seized my hand and shook it, shouting over the roar of the Land Rover engine, *"Yesalaam Guad. Yesalaam Guad."*

He was shaking the hand that had shaken the hand of John F. Kennedy.

We two, there on the highlands of Africa, as far away as one could possibly be from Washington and the White House Rose Garden, shared a moment, were connected by the death of a martyred president and his enduring legacy, the Peace Corps.

John Coyne (Ethiopia 1962-64) was an English teacher in Addis Ababa. He is a novelist and the editor of *Going Up Country: Travel Essays by Peace Corps Writers*. He is also the founding editor of *RPCV Writers & Readers*, a newsletter for and about Peace Corps writers.

Washington, D.C.

Everything I Have in Life, I Owe to Peace Corps

by Jon Keeton

In Fiji a few years ago, I was vaguely aware that the assistant manager of the hotel seemed interested in who I was. As I checked out, he approached and inquired if I was with Peace Corps. When I answered yes, he asked if we could sit down for a minute in the lounge. As he settled somewhat nervously into the deep sofa, he said quietly, "Everything I have in life I owe to Peace Corps." My eyes instantly misted, but I could make out that his had also. I asked him to tell me his story. I still remember each word.

He started by saying that he had been a very poor boy in a village when two Peace Corps Volunteers arrived to teach in his school. They showed him some special attention and let him earn a little money by doing their laundry. When they left, they continued to offer some assistance for his schooling. He finished: "Now I have this good job. My wife has a good job in the government. We have two children in good schools. I own a car. I'm successful.

Everything I have in life, I owe the Peace Corps."

Catching my breath, I told him that so few Volunteers know what they had contributed, and if I could, I would try to contact those two. It would be the first thing that I would do when I got home. "Who were they?" To my amazement, I knew one of them: David Downs.

Back in my office calling David was the first thing I did. Playing on a line of the time, I said, "David, I'm going to make your day." After I told him about his student, he replied, "You've made my year."

David Downs is not the only returned Peace Corps Volunteer who had had his year made by such a tale told by a former student.

I recently received a letter from a student I knew in Thailand who is now a senior level educational administor in Thailand. A succession of Volunteers helped him. He came from a poor village and entered a temple to relieve family pressures but somehow knew he wanted to learn English. He met his first Volunteer at a train station where he approached foreigners to try a few words of English. In his monk's robes, he was an intriguing sight. A health Volunteer by the name of Chris offered him help. She passed him along to Steve and Barbara, who got him started in a good school. I played a role, as did Tracy. Saard now credits all of us with his success. Probably only I, however, have the satisfaction of knowing how richly our efforts have contributed to his life and, in turn, to Thailand. I would love to tell Chris what she started that day at the Lampang station.

Former Peace Corps Director Loret Ruppe used to return from trips overseas with wonderful tales about government leaders who gave a Volunteer credit for their success in life.

The current director, Carol Bellamy, tells of shortly before making her first trip to Africa she met the President of Niger at the Peace Corps office and learned that three of his top aides had been educated by Peace Corps Volunteers.

And it is not only presidential aides who have been educated by the Peace Corps. The current Presidents of Eritrea, Ghana and Uganda were all taught by Peace Corps Volunteers.

And it is not only presidents and aides to presidents who have had their lives changed because of the Peace Corps.

John Pettit, a Volunteer in Ethiopia during the 1960s, helped one of his young female students in the village school where he was teaching by paying her way to a secondary school. He did it because she was bright child and he knew that with a little help, and more education, she could be an outstanding student and have a career beyond the certainty of marrying young and remaining behind in her remote village.

Years later, John met his former student, now a married woman with a family and career of her own, in California where she was living.

She immediately asked him one question, a question that, I'm sure, had been burning in her mind all those years: "Why did you help me?"

Why, she wanted to know, had he changed her life forever by his small gesture of goodwill.

Like most Volunteers who have helped students over the three decades of the Peace Corps, John Pettit did not have an easy answer, beyond saying that he had recognized her abilities and wanted to help. More than that, I guessed, he had wanted, as most Volunteers do, to leave something behind, a tangible result of having been in this country to do service.

Volunteers teach and heal and organize. They build schools, and cooperatives, and fish ponds. And when their tours are over, few are lucky enough to know what tangible results they have left behind.

Will Mike Tidwell's *Ponds of Kalambayi* be there if he returns? Perhaps not. But the people of Kalambayi, especially Ilunga, will remember Michel Tidwell, and the fish ponds he helped build for two years of his young life.

When Volunteers leave a country behind, they are not totally gone from memory. An echo lingers. As Carol Severance says, Peace Corps stories in Micronesia are told and retold and everyone everywhere has tales to tell. It is not only the tales, but the record of achievement, the lives altered and improved.

How many lives have Volunteers made better in countries around the world? The multiplication factors run on and on. They're doing so now as you read this. Begin with 140,000 as the number of former Volunteers and let your imagination ratchet up.

Jon Keeton (Thailand 1965-67) started his Peace Corps tour in a small Thai town as an English supervisor. His staff positions include Country Director in Korea and Regional Director for North Africa, Near East, Asia and Pacific. With a B.A. in history from Berkeley and an M.A. from Columbia. He takes particular delight in having negotiated Peace Corps' entry into Central Europe and the former Soviet Union.

Is Peace Corps Right for You?

How to Become
A Competitive Candidate

Skills Needed for Peace Corps Programs

Agriculture:

Two- or four-year degree, or two to five years' experience.

Agribusiness
Agricultural Ed.
Animal Husbandry
Crop Extension
Environmental
Park/Wildlife Mgmt.

Agricultural Econ.
Agronomy
Animal Science
Environmental Ed.
Sci.Forestry
Soil Science

Skilled Trades:

Vocational/Technical Education or Industrial Arts Degree.
Two to five years professional work can be substituted.

Auto Mechanics
Carpentry
Electricians
Machining
Metal Working
Welding

Cabinet Making
Diesel Mechanics
Gen. Construction
Masonry
Plumbing

Professional Services:

Bachelor's degree or appropriate certification, and/or significant experience.

Business	Civil Engineering
Dietetics	Env. Engineering
HealthHealth Education	Hydrology
Medical Technology	Nursing
Nutrition	

Education:

Bachelor's degree or appropriate certification; teaching experience preferred but not always required.

Biology	Chemistry
Elementary Ed.	English
General Science	Mathematics
Physics	Secondary Ed.
Special Ed.	TEFL/TESOL

Becoming a Peace Corps Volunteer today can be a challenge . . . but it *is* possible to be selected if you develop the skills and experience required for an assignment. Some people will meet the basic requirements based on their degrees and/or work experience; other candidates are successful by developing and gaining skills and experience through activities outside of work or school in addition to their degree. If you do not have the skills listed on the next page, you *can* still become a Peace Corps volunteer:

**If you're
interested in:**

You will need:

English Teaching

BA/BS any discipline with 6 to 12
months of ESL tutoring experi
ence. The tutoring must have been
done within the past 4 years in a
structured program that provides
pre-service training. It also must
be to a student(s) at least 12 years
old, and must take place at least 10
hours a month. French can also
make you more competitive.

**Health & Nutrition
Extension**

Minimum of 3 months experience
in planning, organizing, counseling
or leadership within the past four
years AND a BA/BS any disci
pline with First Aid, EMT or
CPR Certificates and/or 3 to 6
months' health experience such as
hospital/clinic experience, Planned
Parenthood counseling, nurse's
aide or emergency room experience. Most requests require either
French or Spanish.

**Agriculture &
Forestry
Extension**

Minimum of 3 months experience
in planning, organizing, counseling
or leadership within the past four
years AND a BA/BS any disci
pline with 6 to 12 months' experi
ence in vegetable gardening,
forestry, greenhouse, or nursery.

Extensive leadership, organizing, or initiative is often required beyond the required minimum. Many applicants have over 5 years gardening experience. Most assignments require French, some require Spanish.

Public Health/ Sanitation

Minimum of 3 months experience in planning, organizing, counseling or leadership within the past four years AND a BA/BS any discipline with 3 to 6 months experience in construction, masonry, carpentry or plumbing. The most competitive applicants have experience working with concrete and building forms. Most requests require either French or Spanish.

Community Services

BA/BS in any discipline with a minimum of 3 months experience in planning, organizing, counseling or leadership within the past four years. This program is extremely competitive. Most current requests require additional experience such as: AIDS counseling, teaching, French or Spanish, medical and mental health counseling.

Some things to keep in mind...

● The above-mentioned experience is the minimum amount required or suggested for competitiveness. In all cases, the more the better. Remember, we cannot guarantee placement.

● Experience in planning, organizing, counseling or leadership within the past four years is crucial to determining an applicant's competitiveness.

● For all Education assignments, the overall quality of the application (e.g., spelling and grammatical errors) will be taken into consideration when determining the competitiveness of the applicant.

● Study of a foreign language is one factor in determining who is competitive. By itself, however, it will not get you into a program (with the exception of a Master's degree in French or another foreign language, which qualifies an applicant for the University English Teaching program). Other factors being equal, applicants who have recently studied French or Spanish are more competitive than those who have not.

Applying to the Peace Corps:

Your Guide to the Process

Applying to the Peace Corps can be exciting, but it can also be challenging. The application process involves essays, letters of recommendation, medical examinations, and interviews. This guide is designed to familiarize you with what can be a lengthy application, screening, and placement process.

Volunteer Projects

Peace Corps overseas programmers work closely with the officials of our host countries to develop Volunteer projects. Countries begin making their requests for Volunteers two years in advance of the beginning of training. Our recruitment offices target their efforts toward populations that will best yield applicants who have skills the countries want.

Timing of Requests

Fall: October—December
Winter: January—March
Spring: April—June
Summer: July—September

Requests are grouped into four seasons depending upon when trainees begin training. We begin the Volunteer delivery process up to nine months in advance of the beginning of a season. For example, for training that begins sometime during the spring season, the screening and placement process begins in August. We identify two candidates for every one trainee who has been requested; thus the process is competitive.

This entire process, including the medical and legal screening, takes from 4 to 12 months depending on your skills, medical and legal situation, and the seasonal demand from our overseas posts for Volunteers with your skills.

Step 1: The Nominating Phase

Your Application

After you submit your application to an area recruitment office, you will be sent a letter confirming the receipt of your application. A recruiter assigned to you will review your application for basic qualifications and will match your skills and interests to a general skill area. All trainee requests are grouped into 60 generic types of assignments, e.g., forestry, fisheries, construction, nursing, nutrition, science teaching. Each assignment area describes the experience or educational background needed to serve as a Peace Corps Volunteer in that assignment area. If you meet these qualifications, you will be sent a list of the assignment areas for which you qualify along with a request for you to schedule an interview.

Your application could be withdrawn from further consideration at this point for any of the following reasons.
- You are not a U.S. citizen.
- You are under 18.
- You are under supervised probation.
- You are or have been involved in intelligence organizations.
- Your particular skills do not match those requested by Peace Corps host countries.
- You have dependents.

Your Interview

Once it has been determined that you meet the qualifications of a particular assignment area, you will be invited for an interview. This usually takes place within two weeks of receipt of your application. During your interview your recruiter will explore your flexibility, adaptability, social sensitivity, cultural awareness, motivation, and commitment to Peace Corps service. Also, you will need to decide whether Peace Corps service is for you. Your recruiter will not nominate you to an assignment area without an expression of genuine commitment on your part to Peace Corps service.

Your Nomination

In addition to your having been interviewed and determined to have the basic skills our host countries want, there must be an open request for someone with your *specific* skills at the time you are available. If there is such an opening, your application competes with others in the recruitment office for that opening. Nomination can be very competitive, especially for liberal arts majors.

If you are chosen to fill the opening, you will be nominated. This means that your recruiter formally submits your name to the Volunteer delivery system. It is important to emphasize that, as a nominee, you are being considered, along with all other nominees in your particular assignment area, for *various* specific country assignments that begin training in that season.

At the time you are nominated your recruiter may be able to tell you the geographic region for which you are being considered—e.g., Africa, Asia, the Pacific—but will not be able to tell you to which specific country you may be invited. Also, remember that our host countries make these requests up to 12 months before training begins. Thus, they are subject to change, often at the last minute. You will

know your specific country of assignment when and if you
receive an invitation.

Your recruiter will notify you when you are nominated.
At that time you will be given an assignment area name and
number. It is also at this point that your references are con-
tacted by mail and your application is forwarded to the
Washington, D.C., Evaluation Division. Shortly after you
are notified of your nomination, you will receive a nomination kit, which includes a letter confirming your nomination
and an explanation of the evaluation process, and forms,
which you must complete and return *immediately* to the
Evaluation Division. At this time you should also contact
your references and urge them to complete the reference
form as soon as possible to avoid delays.

What You Should Do During the Nominating Phase

- Respond to the request to schedule an interview as
  soon as possible.
- Upon notification of nomination, contact references and urge them to complete the reference
  form as soon as possible.
- Complete and return all forms in the nomination
  kit as soon as possible.

Note regarding your medical condition: *Your medical
history page remains sealed in its envelope until you are
nominated and your package is sent on to the Evaluation
Division in Washington, D.C. The screening process may be
delayed or your placement options severely limited or elim-
inated altogether if you have certain medical conditions
that may jeopardize your health overseas. Please review the
Medical Information for Applicants sheet to assess your
chances of being medically cleared.*

If you have any questions or need advice on anything

during your application process, please contact your recruiter:

Recruiter's Name: _____

Phone Number: _____

Assignment Area Name: _____

Assignment Area Number:_____

Date Nominated: _____

Step 2: The Qualifying Phase

Your Application

Once you are nominated, your application and a summary of your interview are sent to the Evaluation Division. You will receive a letter from Evaluation stating that your file has been received. Your evaluator reviews your application to make sure that your qualifications match the assignment area skill requirements and checks for clarity, accuracy, and completeness.

Your References

Evaluators also collect and review references. It is important that your references send their forms in without delay.

Your Medical History

You must be qualified medically and dentally. You will receive a letter from the Office of Medical Services notifying you of this clearance. The purpose of the clearance system is to insure that you can perform your assignment without jeopardizing your health. The medical qualification process has two possible tracks, pre-invitational and post-invitational.

As soon as the Evaluation Division receives your file,

the sealed envelope containing your medical page is opened by an evaluator and, when necessary, reviewed by a screening nurse. If you have no major medical problems, you are processed routinely. This means that you will receive the necessary papers for your physical after you are invited to a particular Peace Corps assignment.

If you have a problem of any medical significance, the medical qualification process will begin at this point. This means you cannot be invited to a program until you have been qualified by the Office of Medical Services. You will receive your medical examination kit at this time. You should schedule your medical examination immediately so that you may be medically qualified as soon as possible. *(You may proceed to the next step—the placement phase—but you cannot be invited until you are medically qualified.)*

All applicants must undergo a physical and dental examination. The results are reviewed by the Office of Medical Services before an applicant can receive medical qualification. Any irregularities must be corrected. It is your responsibility to provide any/all medical information required to determine your medical suitability. Up to prescribed limitations, Peace Corps pays for your physical and dental examination, but we cannot pay for corrective health care or procedures, or for special evaluations.

Your Legal Information Page

Only applicants who meet the standards of eligibility established by Congress and Peace Corps may be invited to enter training for a Volunteer assignment. If any of the following situations applies to you, your application will be put on *legal hold* and reviewed by the Legal Liaison. Further documentation on these issues will be required and the Legal Liaison will either clear or retire your file based on the content of those additional documents. Please note that the following circumstances do not necessarily disqualify you from Peace Corps service but require further attention and documentation.

- Common law marriages, serving without spouse, or divorced
- Dependents under 18
- Previous convictions
- Student loans (except Perkins loans and National Direct Student Loans)
- Financial obligations (e.g., home mortgage payments, child support)
- Bankruptcy
- Association with intelligence activity
- Application on file with intelligence agency
- Current obligations with Armed Forces, National Guard or Reserve
- Impending legal proceedings involving the applicant

Your Nomination

If you meet the skill and suitability requirements of requesting countries, your evaluator will qualify your application and send it on to the Placement Office. If you do not have all of your references or any other requested information in, if your fingerprints are illegible, or if you have a medical or legal hold, the evaluation process may be delayed. Your application may also be rejected if you do not meet the skill and suitability requirements.

If your references respond promptly, the evaluation process generally takes five to seven weeks. If all goes well, Evaluation will send you a letter stating that you are qualified for Peace Corps service. *(Please remember that medical qualification is a separate process from suitability qualification. It is possible to be found suitability qualified and medically not qualified, and vice versa).* Your application is then forwarded to the Placement Office for further consideration and matching to specific country programs.

Things You Should Do During the Qualifying Phase

●   Make sure that your references have completed and sent in their recommendations.

●   Respond as quickly as you can to requests for further information.

●   Make sure that the Evaluation Division has your most current address.

If you have any changes to your application (e.g., address changes, work history) or any questions about this step, please contact the Evaluation Division directly at 1-800-424-8580 ext. 2218, or, in the metropolitan Washington, D.C. area, 202-606-2080.

Evaluator's Name: _____

Phone Number: _____

Date Qualified _____

Step 3: The Placement Phase

The Placement Office is divided into four skill desks:
1. Agriculture, Forestry, and Fisheries
2. Professional and Technical Trades
3. Health
4. Education

Each skill desk has two or three placement specialists who review and select applicants for specific Volunteer assignments. After your application arrives at the appropriate skill desk in the Placement Office, it is again reviewed for suitability and technical competence—this time against country-specific criteria. Placement specialists make the final decision to invite or not to invite a candidate to training. The process is competitive and is designed to ensure that Peace Corps Volunteers have not only the technical that Peace Corps Volunteers have not only the technical skills needed for their assignments but also the personal qualities necessary to work successfully in specific Peace Corps assignments. They also take into consideration motivation, maturity, flexibility, and interpersonal skills.

Though you are initially nominated into a general skill area, all of your skills are taken into consideration in determining whether (and to where) you receive an invitation. Because of the competitive nature of the placement process, it can be lengthy. Your application may also be delayed due to a legal or medical hold. This phase may take anywhere from one to nine months.

If you receive an invitation, you will have ten days to respond. The invitation packet also includes a Volunteer Assignment Description, more forms to complete (i.e., passport and visa applications), and an invitation booklet that will guide you through the next few steps.

If you are beginning the medical screening process at the point of invitation, your invitation will also include a medical kit. You should schedule your medical and dental examinations immediately. You must receive a letter of qualification from the Office of Medical Services before traveling to your pre-departure orientation.

Once you have accepted an invitation, Peace Corps will send you the specific information you will need to prepare for training. The Country Desk Officer will send you a packet of detailed information about your host country and a description of your training. The packet will include a recommended clothing list and a country-specific bibliography. Later you will receive instructions with details about time, date, and location of your pre-departure orientation. The Travel Office will send you airline tickets if you have been medically and dentally qualified, and soon you will be on your way!

Things You Should Do During the Placement Phase

● If on medical or legal hold, send in all requested information in a timely manner.

● Respond as quickly as you can to requests for further information.

● Make sure the Placement Skill Desk has your most current address and phone number to assure you are receiving all requests for information promptly.

If you have any changes to your application (e.g., address changes, work history) or any questions, contact the appropriate skill desk at 1-800-424-8580.

Agriculture/Forestry/Fisheries
ext. 2216, 2217

Professional and Technical Trades
ext. 2253, 2254

Health and Unique Skills
ext. 2235, 2238

Education
ext. 2213

Placement Officer's Name: _____

Skill Desk: _____

Phone Number:_____